TIME
LIFE
BOOKS
®

LIFE WORLD LIBRARY
LIFE NATURE LIBRARY
LIFE SCIENCE LIBRARY
THE LIFE HISTORY OF THE UNITED STATES
GREAT AGES OF MAN
TIME-LIFE LIBRARY OF ART
TIME READING PROGRAM
INTERNATIONAL BOOK SOCIETY

LIFE Pictorial Atlas of the World
The Epic of Man
The Wonders of Life on Earth
The World We Live In
The World's Great Religions
The LIFE Book of Christmas
LIFE's Picture History of Western Man
The LIFE Treasury of American Folklore
America's Arts and Skills
300 Years of American Painting
The Second World War
LIFE's Picture History of World War II
Picture Cook Book
LIFE Guide to Paris

LIFE WORLD LIBRARY
MEXICO

LIFE WORLD LIBRARY

MEXICO

by William Weber Johnson
and The Editors of LIFE

TIME INCORPORATED   NEW YORK

COVER: Indians in homespun
rest on a street in Jamiltepec
during a fiesta. Like many
country people throughout
Mexico, they speak little Spanish.

ABOUT THE WRITER

William Weber Johnson first came to know Mexico on college vacations,
when he wandered extensively through the land on foot, horseback and
riverboat. A native of Illinois, he has worked for Time Inc. as a staff
writer and reporter. He was a combat correspondent during World War II,
later serving as chief of the TIME-LIFE bureaus in Mexico City and
Buenos Aires. A frequent visitor to Mexico, he has known almost all of
the country's eminent men of the past 20 years. Johnson is the author
of numerous articles on Mexico and the American Southwest as well as
of "Captain Cortés Conquers Mexico," a children's history of the Con-
quistadors. His book, "Kelly Blue," a biography of Harold Osman Kelly,
the Texas primitive painter, was published in 1960. Johnson is now a
professor of journalism at the University of California at Los Angeles.

Contents

TIME-LIFE BOOKS

EDITOR
Norman P. Ross
EXECUTIVE EDITOR
Maitland A. Edey
TEXT DIRECTOR   ART DIRECTOR
Jerry Korn   Edward A. Hamilton
CHIEF OF RESEARCH
Beatrice T. Dobie
Assistant Text Director: Harold C. Field
Assistant Art Director: Arnold C. Holeywell
Assistant Chiefs of Research:
Monica O. Horne, Martha Turner

•

PUBLISHER
Rhett Austell
General Manager: Joseph C. Hazen Jr.
Planning Director: Frank M. White
Business Manager: John D. McSweeney
Circulation Director: Joan D. Manley
Publishing Board: Nicholas Benton, Louis Bronzo,
James Wendell Forbes, John S. Wiseman

LIFE MAGAZINE

EDITOR: Edward K. Thompson
MANAGING EDITOR: George P. Hunt
PUBLISHER: Jerome S. Hardy

LIFE WORLD LIBRARY

SERIES EDITOR: Oliver E. Allen
Editorial Staff for *Mexico:*
Assistant Editor: Jay Brennan
Designer: Ben Schultz
Chief Researcher: Grace Brynolson
Researchers: Irene Ertugrul, Nancy Jones, Helen Turvey,
Linda Wolfe, Gwyneth Barger, Jean Sulzberger

EDITORIAL PRODUCTION
Color Director: Robert L. Young
Copy Staff: Marian Gordon Goldman, Ann S. Lang, Dolores A. Littles
Picture Bureau: Margaret K. Goldsmith, Sue Bond
Art Assistants: James D. Smith, Richard Forte

The text for this book was written by William Weber Johnson, the
picture essays by Walter Karp and David S. Thomson. The following
individuals and departments of Time Inc. were helpful in producing
the book: Ralph Crane, Eliot Elisofon, Dmitri Kessel and Leonard
McCombe, LIFE staff photographers; Mathilde Camacho of LIFE EN
ESPAÑOL; Richard Oulahan of LIFE; Doris O'Neil, Chief of the LIFE
Picture Library; Richard M. Clurman, Chief of the TIME-LIFE News
Service; and Peter Draz, Chief of the Bureau of Editorial Reference.

Introduction

The tides of history run with unsuspected power and depth. Henry Adams observed that there is a rate of acceleration in the universe. Only in recent years have we realized that this acceleration particularly grips the countries of Latin America—which we wishfully assumed were at slack tide, although we realized that Europe, Asia and Africa were at the flood.

It is always easier to be informed about the familiar nations of Europe or dead empires whose history stands still for our leisured inspection than to work to understand the present. But political and social forces can burst through to significance as dramatically as the volcano of Parícutin erupted through a peaceful farm in Michoacán, Mexico, in 1943, to grow in a few years into a mountain.

Mexico is a future power forming under our eyes. By the year 2000 it is expected to have a population of more than 75 million. *If* both Mexico and the U.S. choose, Mexico can be a most valuable bridge between the northern and southern families of the Western Hemisphere.

In this book the Editors of LIFE do the United States a service by placing in perspective the past, present and future of Mexico for the hitherto casually informed U.S. reader.

As this book points out, geography and history have created difficulties beyond belief for Mexico. Many languages and many people still blend in the volcano of the country's pride and nationalism. One hundred and fifty years after the break with Spain, Mexico continues the struggle to complete its Revolution and to integrate all its people through a common nationalism and a common way of life.

Mr. Johnson's text makes clear—and it is one of the facts of life which the U.S. must understand—that Mexico is working to these ends through a form of government different from our own, despite the fact that both nations refer to themselves as "democracies." The chapter on Mexico's one-party system spells out why our next door neighbor's "democracy" is not our kind of democracy.

Every Latin American nation is going to work out its destiny in its own way. If we are to be intelligent as the leader of the Western world, it behooves us to know where these nations are headed on their own, rather than try to force them into a mold we would like. We must not lose our heads or hearts if they have ideas of their own.

Seven hundred thousand American tourists annually go to Mexico to buy its beautiful handicraft, to wonder at its dramatic scenery, to be charmed by its cultivated and dignified people. But not enough U.S. citizens perceive what U.S. policy makers have to understand about the primal political and social energies that have made and are continually remaking modern Mexico. This book will, I hope, help U.S. citizens to comprehend the Mexico with which the U.S. of this generation must live.

For nearly four years I traveled into every state and province of Mexico with a wife and two children, savoring its life on every level. We felt the heartbeat of this endearing people—from humble but dignified *campesinos* to distinguished political leaders and proud, brilliant intellectuals. They have been our friends; we shall always be theirs. Viva Mexico!

ROBERT C. HILL
former U.S. Ambassador to Mexico

Sunday picnickers from Mexico City cluster among the maguey plants of Chapultepec Park. A 1,300-acre sanctuary for the city's three

The Kaleidoscopic Air

1

million people, the park is a natural woodland spruced up with shaded walks and bridle paths. It was once a favorite dueling ground.

THE oldest city on the continent of North America, splendid and squalid, sprawls broadly on a high, volcano-girt plateau where the air is thin and clear, the wind capricious, the sunlight blinding, the shadows deep and chilling. The wind spins dust devils across the dry bed of the lake that once surrounded what is now Mexico City. It twists plumes of smoke above the mountainside *milpas* where Indians grow maize in the old ways, burning the fields and breaking the ground with a pointed stick. It piles cumulus clouds majestically over the Sierra of Ajusco and the Desert of the Lions.

The brilliant light sparkles over the ice-clad peaks of Popocatepetl and Iztaccihuatl. It flashes on multicolored mosaic walls and on the cold steel and glass façades of skyscrapers. It washes softly over the gray and red lava sides of colonial buildings, over the tumbled blocks of ancient pyramids. It sharpens the details of old stone carvings, those of suffering Christian saints and monstrous pre-Christian gods alike. It touches with fire the roses and gladioli that bloom in abundance in public gardens and the *bugambilia* that clings everywhere—to the high stone walls that conceal mansions of magnificence and to the humble adobe walls of miserable tenements where humans live in antlike colonies. It washes over the nearly nude body of a movie star, stretched languorously beside a pool of blue water in a garden of bright flowers and lush greenery, and it casts deep shadows in the lined face of an aged Indian woman who sells wax matches and cigarettes from a tray near the equestrian statue of King Charles IV of Spain—a statue which, Mexican attitudes toward royalty being what they are, is known simply as *El Caballito,* the little horse.

ALONG avenues that once were causeways connecting the old Aztec island capital of Tenochtitlán with the mainland, the traffic boils and surges. Buses careen through the streets, with passengers clinging to roof, bumper and doorstep. Decrepit trucks, monstrously overloaded, grind their way through the maze. Taxis painted in heathenish splendor race each other, the drivers shouting obscenities or exchanging hand signals and whistles of unmistakable meaning. Antique Ford races antique Fiat. Sleek Mercedes glides beside sleek Cadillac, the conveyance of bankers and politicians. A delivery boy teeters by on a bicycle, a great basket of bakery goods balanced on his head. A *cargador,* or porter, with a stack of handmade chairs piled high on his back shuffles along in the stream of traffic, steadily maintaining the "coyote step" that keeps him from falling forward on his face under the weight. An Indian drags a squealing pig at the end of a frayed rope; another drives a flock of undersized turkeys along the gutter, inches away from death under car wheels. Small newsboys wave their papers like flags, shouting of crimes of passion, disasters on the road, scandals in the republic and the latest results of *box* and *beisbol.*

Braked tires scream. Accelerated motors roar through broken mufflers. Ambulance sirens mingle with the offkey music of curbside barrel organs. Full-throated jukeboxes blare songs of outraged love from saloons. Soap operas, singing commercials and traditional ballads shriek from a hundred radio and television sets, each with the volume turned on full. From the sidewalks come the cries of shoeshine boys and lottery-ticket sellers—"Five hundred thousand for today, chief; I have your lucky number." Office girls, immaculately dressed, every hair in place, their eyes carefully shadowed, walk along, arm in arm, their voices like the chirping of birds.

The sounds are strident and arhythmic except for the soft, steady slap-slap of women shaping maize dough into *tortillas,* most universal and ancient of Mexican foods; and the aroma of stone-ground meal is never far away. Nor, for that matter, is the smell of flowers—carnations, gardenias, dahlias, roses, geraniums, daisies, marigolds—carried through the streets in baskets or bundles on the backs of Indian women; of dust, strong tobacco and faulty drains; of French perfumes and bouquets of herbs, drying in the hot sunlight; of charcoal fires, of good Mexican coffee and of the mysterious mixtures, always strong with chili, simmering in clay pots over tiny braziers, tended by country women sitting placidly on the sidewalk, their skirts outspread, their black hair braided with bright yarn.

THE air of Mexico City is nervous, vital, hectic, dynamic, eclectic and kaleidoscopic. The stranger can find almost anything he seeks, except that he will look in vain for his preconceived notion of a Mexican—the little man seated under a tree, hat over eyes, face on knees, taking a siesta. He cannot be found, although the observant stranger may see a *cargador* who has carried a hundred-pound load on his back over 40 miles of mountain roads, lying on the grass and gasping, trying to fill his aching lungs with the thin air of the high plateau. The charming air of *mañana* or tomorrow, of procrastination, which the guidebooks say pervades life "south of the border," also is missing. But tomorrow's air is there, all right. So is the air of the day after tomorrow, of yesterday and the day before yesterday, but above all it is the air of today, this very minute, and hurry up about it.

Colonial buildings, graciously ornate, their hand-carved stone façades like ancient filigree, blaze with light and whir with the sound of electronic computing machines. At the National University, oldest educational institution on the North American continent, 75,000 students rush from class to class in buildings that are breathtakingly modern, their walls gleaming with mosaic murals by Mexico's great artists—murals telling the story of the nation's dark legends, its agonizing conflicts and its hopeful future. From any one of the buildings students can look across the lava-bed area known as the Pedregal toward the pyramid of Cuicuilco, which antedates the era of the Aztecs as much as the era of the Aztecs antedates their own. Beneath the crude outlines of that pyramid lie the ruins of another, and below that the ruins of still another, wrapped in mystery.

In the middle of the city stands the great Centro Médico, a staggering complex of research centers, laboratories, hospitals where wage-earning Mexicans can come for free medical or surgical care, and vast auditoriums where the world's learned men of medicine can meet and discuss the advancement of medical science. And a few blocks away one can still visit a *curandera* who diagnoses illness by rubbing the patient's body with an egg, then breaking the egg in a pottery dish and studying the form assumed by the broken yolk. She may prescribe nasturtium leaves plastered on the temples to reduce fever, or rosemary for skin eruptions, or an amulet to guarantee love.

Mansions of the new rich, with high walls enclosing a world of high-fidelity music, electric blenders, swimming pools and U.S.-made plumbing, are sometimes built on what may have been burial grounds or kitchen middens for one of the old cultures. Digging turns up a supply of idols and primitive cooking utensils, shaped from clay or carved from stone. Just beyond the wall a *paracaidista*—"parachutist" or squatter family—may be living in a hut, preparing its food with newer but otherwise identical utensils fashioned of clay or stone, while the children play with small clay dolls that are not unlike the little idols.

Take a seat anywhere in Mexico City; if you sit there long enough you will see some of Mexico's multiple faces, hear some of its many tongues. Sit in the Zócalo, heart of the Mexican world as it was of the Aztec world, the plaza where the great decisive battle was fought between the ruthlessly ambitious men of the Old World and the fierce, demon-ridden men of the New. Or in the strikingly lovely Paseo de la Reforma, much of it planned by the European dreamer Maximilian, but named for the upheaval that put him before a firing squad. Or near one of the great modern markets where you can buy glowing fruit from the tropics, glistening shrimp from Campeche, fat oysters from Guaymas, rayon ribbons, plastic tableware or charms against the evil eye and wind stones to protect you from sinister airs. Or in the thieves' market at Lagunilla, where you will be offered gore-speckled figures of tortured saints, looted from old churches. Or in the Plaza of Santo Domingo, where the Inquisition

MEXICAN SPANISH

Spanish, the language of Mexico's conquerors, blended with Nahuatl, the tongue of the Aztecs, to produce Mexican Spanish, the *lengua nacional*, which is spoken with an unmistakable Mexican lilt. Nahuatl words are commonly used for foods, beverages, household implements, birds and animals. Some, by way of Spanish, have found their way into common use in English and other tongues. Examples:

NAHUATL	ENGLISH
Ahuacatl	Avocado
Cacahuatl	Cacao, cocoa
Chocólatl	Chocolate
Coyotl	Coyote
Chictli	Chicle
Chilli	Chili
Mizquitl	Mesquite
Ocelotl	Ocelot
Peyotl	Peyote
Tamalli	Tamale
Tequilan	Tequila
Tomatl	Tomato

held its cruel deliberations and where today *evangelistas*, letter writers with obsolete type-writers, perform for a few pennies a service of love: if you describe the situation they will write for you an appealing love letter, couched in the most courtly Spanish. Or in Chapultepec Park under the ahuehuete trees that were tall even in the days of Netzahualcóyotl, the 15th Century poet king (". . . the obscurity of the night but serves to reveal the brilliance of the stars. . . ."). Or in the Alameda, among the flowers and near the monument to the great 19th Century reformer Benito Juárez ("Peace is respect for the rights of others").

You will see women in New York and Paris fashions and women in huipils, the standard outergarment of Mexican Indian women for a thousand years; the elaborately embroidered costumes from Tehuantepec; the rusty black of Spanish widowhood; and everywhere the *rebozo*, the all-purpose shawl which serves as head covering, shoulder wrap, market basket and cradle. To the anthropologist the method of draping the *rebozo* is a sure indication of regional origin, as is the color of the yarn or ribbon woven into the women's shiny black braids. There will be men in tight trousers and short jackets, heavily brocaded in the *charro* tradition; men in white pajamalike cotton suits from the warmer states of Morelos and Guerrero; men in low-crowned, beribboned hats from Michoacán and men in high-crowned hats from Veracruz, voluble and good-natured; Chamula Indians, barelegged; grim-faced Yaquis in the gray-green uniform of the Mexican army; men in severe black suits and sunglasses; and the capital's poverty-stricken *pelados*, or peeled ones, lowest of the low in the economic order, in their precariously worn rags.

THEY will be speaking as great a variety of languages as can be heard in any of the world's capitals: the slurring slang of Mexico City itself, full of double meanings and thinly veiled abuse; lisping Castilian; precise English; *pocho* Spanish from the northern border country, an execrable mixture of bad Spanish and bad English; the Spanish of Mexican poets, pure, sonorous and full of glittering images; or Nahuatl, most prevalent of Mexico's 50-odd surviving Indian languages and dialects, sounding vaguely Oriental; or Otomí, Huastec, Totonaco, Huichol, Tzotzil or Tarahumara. Two Indians from the state of Oaxaca may try to converse; but one is Mixtec and his words for man, woman, father and mother are, respectively, *yee*, *nahadzehe*, *dzutu* and *dzehe*, while the other uses Zapotec words for the same, *beni*, *benigonnaa*, *bixoce* and *xiñaagaxana*. There are almost one million Indians in Mexico who speak no Spanish whatsoever and who sometimes cannot cope even with the Indian language spoken in a nearby village. "To understand Mexico," runs a wry saying, "you must understand Indians, for we are an Indian country. And who understands Indians?"

At the Plaza of the Three Cultures in Mexico City—a handsome park containing the ruins of an Aztec ceremonial center, a well-restored colonial church, and Mexico's new and very modern Ministry of Foreign Relations—a monument marks the site of one of the final battles between the Aztecs and the Spaniards with this inscription: "It was neither triumph nor defeat—it was instead the painful birth of the mestizo people who are Mexico today."

MEXICO is a mestizo nation, a people of mixed blood (in colonial days the government recognized four classes—Spaniards, Creoles, Indians and Negroes—plus 16 specified mixed-blood types). A Mexican is many more things, both racially and temperamentally.

He may be a person of formidable intelligence and knowledge, multilingual, his culture rich and highly glossed. Or he may be one of the 30 per cent of Mexicans who can neither read nor write.

He may be devoutly Catholic, or he may be bitterly anticlerical, full to bursting with complaints about the iniquities which Mexico officially lays at the door of the Church. Or he may be, as many Mexicans are, both Catholic *and* anticlerical.

He may boast of unadulterated Spanish lineage, speaking scornfully of his fellow countrymen as "these Indians," or he may assure you —with equal pride and as little accuracy—that he is pure Indian himself. Or, having acquired a business suit and factory-made shoes, he may confide: "I used to be an Indian."

He may be wealthy to a degree that is rare in the 20th Century; he may have a palace in the Lomas of Chapultepec, a ranch in Puebla, a weekend house in Cuernavaca, a beach cottage in Acapulco, an apartment in Beverly Hills, a suite at the Waldorf, a fleet of Cadillacs, an army of servants. Or he may suffer from the kind of hopeless, aching poverty that in Mexico is never more than an arm's length away.

HE may desire wealth and work for it with single-minded dedication and ruthlessness, or he may be wholly indifferent to it, indifferent in the way that both his Indian ancestors and the early Christians were.

He may have the remarkable instincts for color and form that place Mexicans among the world's great natural artists, or he may be guilty of the inordinate bad taste that a hybrid civilization is so likely to produce.

He may be open, extroverted, extravagantly convivial; he is more often merely polite and well-mannered, while remaining as closed and inscrutable underneath as an Aztec idol.

He may discuss a business deal with hardheaded acumen and with great and knowing attention to detail—and at the last minute suggest a postponement in the signing of the contract, not because there is anything wrong, but "because the wind is too strong today."

He may fancy himself a friend of foreigners and may adopt foreign manners of speaking and dress; but he will just as often say with some bitterness that Mexico has had nothing but trouble at the hands of foreigners—Spanish, French, English and Yankee.

He may delight in telling stories of his own government's ineptitude, spinning out tales of corruption, political irregularity and scandal; but he may just as often bristle with anger if the same subjects are broached in the presence of foreigners.

He may take sides in the cold war. Or he may say as a Yucatecan, coming from the most isolated part of Mexico, is supposed to have said: "Let them drop the big bomb and destroy the world; I can always go back to Mérida."

Mexicans joke about the different kinds of Mexicans.

Regiomontanos from the state of Nuevo León and the bustling industrial city of Monterrey, they will say, are generally humorless and uniformly stingy. *Veracruzanos* from the tropical Gulf Coast are great lovers of food, drink, music and dancing and, with the best intentions, are the most foul-mouthed of all Mexicans. *Poblanos,* the people from Puebla, are supposed to be mean and treacherous; an old jingle runs "monkey, parrot or *Poblano*—do not touch them with your *mano* [hand]." Yucatecans are considered naïve, but naïve in an ingratiating way, the butt of a thousand jokes. Jalisco, the source of the best *mariachi* music, is supposed to produce the most *macho*, or masculine, of Mexican men, rugged fellows, adept at riding wild horses, roping cattle, singing serenades and defending their honor. A man from Jalisco, in typical fashion, says, "In my country we are strong and rough, we are all pure *macho*." A Yucatecan answers, "Well, *señor*, in Yucatán half of us are *macho* and the other half are women and we are very content that way."

IN a more serious vein, Mexicans are greatly preoccupied with, and generally puzzled by, the Mexican character—how it functions and why Mexicans behave the way they do. It is a favorite conversational topic not only among observers of the country, but among Mexicans themselves. "The Mexican," writes essayist Ramón Xirau, "questions the sense of his own being, of his own nature. Who else wonders about the meaning of his own existence?"

There are certain areas of agreement and uniformity. The Mexicans are a strong family people. The family is a closed unit against the world. Women, for the most part, lead lives that are carefully cloistered and protected. Men enjoy more freedom. The *casa chica,* or little house—the separate extramarital establishment for the husband's pleasure—is common at all levels of society, but it does not impair the sanctity of the home. Children are reared in a tight cocoon of discipline and affection, with usually agreeable results. Essayist Charles Flandrau, observing the pleasant manners and uncomplaining obedience of Mexican children, suggested that all the world's children should be required to be Mexican until the age of 15.

There is a fascination with the macabre, with the circumstances and trappings of death. This may be a logical development from the executions of the Spanish Inquisition (which functioned in Mexico until the early 19th Century) and from the human sacrifices of Indian Mexico. One of the nation's most popular holidays is the Day of the Dead, when deceased forebears are honored ceremoniously and children are given candy skulls to eat.

There is a love of fiesta, of religious festivals or patriotic celebrations, of market days and family anniversaries.

There is a highly developed sense of humor, wry, cynical, satirical and unsparing. Although the Mexican takes himself as seriously as do his Spanish cousins and his Latin American brothers, he is more ready than the others to make a joke about it.

AND there is an almost universal stoicism that is part Spanish but more Indian. Writes Octavio Paz, Mexican poet, essayist and diplomat: "Stoicism is the highest Mexican virtue—military or political. Our history is replete with speeches and episodes which demonstrate the indifference of our heroes to pain and danger. From childhood on we are taught to accept defeat with dignity . . . and if we can't all be stoics . . . at least we can try to be patient, resigned, long-suffering. . . . Much more than to victory we thrill to fortitude in the face of adversity." Paz and others have pointed out that most of Mexico's great heroes were, in the end, failures: Cuauhtémoc, Hidalgo, Morelos, Madero, Zapata. All are loved as much for their disastrous ends as for their principles.

One of the early lessons in history taught to all Mexican children is the story of the *Niños Héroes,* the six boy heroes of the 1846-1848 war with the United States. The six—Juan de la Barrera, Francisco Márquez, Fernando Montes de Oca, Agustín Melgar, Vicente Súarez and Juan Escutia—were cadets of the Military College who made a suicidal last stand on the heights of Chapultepec against the invading Yankee army, shouting with their dying breath, *"Viva México! Viva el Colegio Militar!"* Mexican history is full of heroism and courage and of greater accomplishment on the field of battle, but no other event reflects quite so accurately the Mexican taste in heroics. The monument to the six young heroes is a national shrine.

YET all Mexicans today are involved in and committed to the very antithesis of hopelessness and stoicism: the Mexican Revolution. This does not refer just to the armed conflict that broke out in 1910 and continued for a decade of desolation and confusion, but more generally to the sociopolitical upheaval that began at that time and now, half a century later, is continuing on a wider and wider social front.

The Mexican Revolution contains traces of old-style socialism, of Marxism and of capitalism, with a strong admixture of Indian customs that prevailed long before the white man knew there was an American continent. In its complex whole it is aimed at solving problems, some of which are peculiarly Mexican but many of which are common in areas of the world that have suffered from backwardness, repression, exploitation and perennial turmoil. It has not, Mexicans readily admit, answered all of Mexico's shortcomings in education, communications, social and political homogeneity and material well-being. But progress is being made and can best be measured against Mexico's tortured past. It is an ingenious and curiously Mexican invention.

"Como México no hay dos," Mexicans like to say—there is no other country like it.

DANGLING TRIO cleans the glass face of a Mexico City skyscraper. Mexico strongly favors ultramodern architecture which dramatically emphasizes glass and concrete.

A Harmony Amid Diversity

No chords are muted in Mexico and no edges are blurred. Everything proclaims itself boldly, whether in the etched shapes of the landscapes, the clean upthrust of modern buildings or in the stark qualities of the people. A millionaire in Mexico does not hide his opulence, nor a poor man his rags: each demands to be seen as he is. In Mexico, even death is not glossed over; on the holiday known as the Day of the Dead it is greeted with festivities. But the total effect is not one of conflict, for the country's sharp and insistent qualities do not clash with one another. Among the flamboyant elements of Mexico, a balanced harmony prevails.

FASHIONABLE WEDDING revives traditional *charro* style, the groom dressed in the elaborate clothes of a 19th Century Mexican rancher and the *charras*, or extra bridesmaids, in old-fashioned dresses and big hats.

NATTY COMEDIAN, Mario Moreno—better known by his stage name of Cantinflas—strolls in London *(left)*. Long an idol to Mexicans, he achieved wider fame through a role in the film *Around the World in 80 Days*.

PURPLE DUSK in Mexico City *(opposite)* is spangled with lights which stretch to the distant mountains. In the foreground is the Alameda, a beautiful small park with fine walks, fountains and centuries-old trees.

VIVID PAST confronts four farmers inspecting the murals in the Cortés palace in Cuernavaca. Painted by Diego Rivera, the murals highlight Mexican history from pre-Conquest days.

GOLDEN ARCH of the Tepotzotlán Convent church shines sumptuously in the morning sun (*left*). In Mexico many old churches boast this kind of astonishingly lavish adornment.

19

MUSIC MAKERS assemble around the local shrine (*opposite*) before striking up their amateur band for a fiesta in Jamiltepec, a remote village in Oaxaca.

MOURNING GIRL, wearing her best shawl, takes flowers to the grave of her infant sister. Resignation to death comes early to Mexico's children.

WADING WOMEN brave the Atoyac River to bring vegetables to the Oaxaca market. Market profits are so meager that few farm people use the nearby toll bridge.

LOOMING VOLCANO, snow-crowned Popocatepetl rises above the church towers of the village of Amecameca to dominate the valleys and hills bordering Mexico City.

A Harsh Landscape To Conquer

IN Mexico the very nature of the land argues against orderly progression and easy solutions to the country's multiple problems. The spectacular landscape is by turns awesome and beautiful, benign and forbidding. It provides an extraordinary challenge to man's ingenuity and energy.

For it is not one land but many. It contains baked deserts where rainfall is almost unknown and tropical forests where rain is measured in feet rather than in inches. It includes sun-scorched sea-level savannas and mile-high tablelands, vast dry canyons that lay bare the entrails of the earth and broad jungle rivers. It enjoys groves of trees heavy with orchids and bromelias, plains of cacti, meadows of alpine flowers and lush valleys rich with mangoes, papaya, melons and sugar cane; it has sterile highlands where impoverished dwellers boil weeds for scant nourishment. It is a country alive with flowers—Mexico has given to the world poinsettias, dahlias, cosmos and marigolds—yet the land's most familiar aspect is one of bare aridity. Maize, known as corn in the United States, is the basic crop, the food upon which the early civilizations were founded. It is the universal staple of the Mexican diet today. To flourish, maize generally requires specialized climatic conditions. Yet within the boundaries of Mexico, in part because of the variety of climate, terrain and soil, some 4,000 native types of maize are believed to have developed through the ages.

Mexico is a vertical country as well as a horizontal one. Its lands lie between sea level and heights of more than three miles. A good half of it lies south of the Tropic of Cancer, but it is a tropical land only in part. The central tableland, the *altiplano*, varies from a mile to a mile and a half in altitude, one of the highest inhabited areas in the world (after Tibet and the Andean countries). The dweller on the tableland has as much in common with the man from the plains of Asia as he has with his own countrymen from the marshy lowlands of Tabasco or the remote tropical beaches of the Costa Chica. The distance between neighboring villages may be no more than four or five miles in a straight line but it may be 20 miles by the only available mule path—and 500 miles in climate. The climates of municipalities which, like Tepoztlán in the state of Morelos, lie almost entirely on mountain slopes, range from temperate in the heights to subtropic in the lowlands, all within the space of a few miles.

THREE great mountain ranges, each of them staggering in size and complexity and virtually impenetrable, divide the country. In the west, the Sierra Madre Occidental constitutes an almost impassable barrier, sealing off the peninsula of Lower California and the state of Sonora from the north central plains of Mexico. To the south, the mountains run to the sea, making land travel impossible along the coast. Where the land mass swings eastward the range becomes the equally impassable Sierra Madre del Sur. This in turn joins the southerly thrust of the Sierra Madre Oriental, a somewhat lesser range but still a forbidding barrier between the coastal plain of the Gulf of Mexico and the interior highlands.

Farther to the south, below the central *altiplano* and the tangle of the various Sierra Madres, the land flattens into the Isthmus of Tehuantepec, a country of high winds. It then rises again into the rugged mountains of Chiapas and the Guatemalan border. To the east lie jungles and intricate networks of little-known rivers that empty on the coasts of Tabasco and Campeche; beyond them are the limestone plains of Yucatán and the forests of Quintana Roo. Throughout the republic are large areas that are still virtually unexplored and mapped only in the most tentative way.

THE story is told—as it has been told of many countries but seldom so fittingly— that soon after the Conquest of Mexico in the 16th Century, a Spanish king, impressed by the quantities of treasure that had flowed into his hands from the mysterious new land in the West, summoned before him a man who had recently returned from New Spain.

"Tell me about our new realm," he commanded. "What is it like?"

The visitor struggled with words and, failing, seized a piece of paper from a table. He crushed it between his hands, rolled it, pressed it again and again until the paper was a crumpled ball, a meaningless complex of ridges, crevices, peaks and depressions.

"There, Your Majesty," he said, "is a map of New Spain."

To the dimensions of breadth and height must be added a third, that of depth. Much of Mexico sits precariously above a great, mysterious subterranean source of geological torments: a volcanic zone that periodically rocks the earth with tremors and creates mountains where none ever existed before. This zone runs roughly across the middle of the country, from Banderas Bay on the Pacific to the Veracruz area on the Gulf Coast. In 1803 Baron von Humboldt, that tireless observer and notetaker, correctly calculated that it was associated with what is now called the Circum-Pacific Ring, a volcanic belt that travels around the periphery of the ocean all the way from Japan. The belt is a potent breeder of violence. Within Mexico it has been, from dimly ancient times, the source of awesome phenomena. Tremendous pressures from within the earth have pushed up the surface in uneven planes along its extent, punctuating the chaos with eruptions of fire and molten rock. The volcanic zone covers nearly 100,000 square miles, an area in which the normal ruggedness of the terrain, compounded by the mountain chain, becomes almost labyrinthine.

There is no precise count on the number of volcanoes, extinct, dormant or active, within Mexico. Only the largest ones are well known. The highest (18,700 feet) is Orizaba or Citlaltepetl on the border between the states of Veracruz and Puebla; its snowy peak catches the first rays of the rising sun while all the rest of Mexico lies in darkness. Then there are Popocatepetl (17,887 feet) and Iztaccihuatl (17,342 feet), which hang brooding over the capital and the central plateau; also noted are Malinche, Cofre de Perote, Nevado de Toluca, Tancítaro and Colima. For every nationally familiar peak there are scores of others that are known and recognized only in their immediate vicinity. The picturesque state of Michoacán has 80-odd volcanoes. The newest of them, Parícutin, broke the surface of a field in 1943 under the eyes of a terrified farmer. Spewing lava and ashes over forests and croplands, Parícutin quickly buried the nearby town of San Juan Parangaricutiro. It grew to a height of 1,700 feet before becoming dormant in 1952.

SEISMOLOGISTS say that Mexico and Central America are part of the world's most active earthquake zone. Tremors are commonplace, and it is sometimes said that Mexico City would long ago have disappeared from the face of the earth were it not cushioned from the worst of the violence by the subterranean sea of mud on which it rests. Despite the cushion, a series of tremors in the summer of 1957 took at least 60 lives in Mexico City and caused property damage of more than $25 million.

Tribal memories of ancient earthquakes and volcanic destruction may have helped develop the fatalism and superstition that made it possible for a handful of Spaniards in the 16th Century to conquer the Aztecs. Aztec mythology told of three earlier epochs, each of which ended in disaster. No one, in fact, knows how many ancient cultures lie buried in the lava beds of Mexico. Tremors and floods of lava may also have played a part in the sometimes inexplicable migrations of the ancient people of Mexico, the sudden termination of highly developed cultures, the abrupt desertion of elaborately wrought cities.

HOW and why mankind first came to a land so inhospitable is still a considerable anthropological puzzle. It has been argued that man originated in Mexico, that he came to it from Plato's Atlantis or from "the lost continent of Mu," that there was a prehistoric migration from the valley of the Nile, that the "Indians" of Mexico were really remnants of the Ten Lost Tribes of Israel or descendants of the Scythians. The most accepted explanation is that the early Americans were Stone Age people from Asia who migrated across the Bering Strait and through the Aleutian Islands between 20,000 and 25,000 years ago. By 10,000 B.C. these primitive Americans were hunting now extinct elephants in the Valley of Mexico, and by 3000 B.C. they were grinding corn between stones, suggesting that theirs was a settled rather than a nomadic life.

Mexico's early civilizations became oriented about this major crop. The systematic raising of maize led to formalization of religion, with prayers and ceremonies for rain, sunlight and other favorable conditions. The necessity of planting, cultivating and harvesting at the right time in turn led to remarkably sophisticated astronomical observations, calendar keeping and mathematics. The Mayas of Mexico had invented the abstract symbol of zero to simplify mathematics long before it was in use in Europe; similarly, the Mayan calendar was older and more efficiently conceived than the Julian calendar used by Europeans at the time of the Conquest of Mexico.

The full extent of the civilization that was established in this tortured land may, in fact,

NAYARIT

HUASTEC

JALISCO

Chupicuaro ▲

Tula ■

TOLTEC

Teotihuacán
Tlatilco ▲

Tajín ●

TOTONAC

Tenochtitlán (Mexico) ■

Cuicuilco ▲

◙ Cholula

COLIMA

Xochicalco ◙

OLMEC

MIXTEC

La Venta ▲

Monte Albán ◈

◙ Mitla

ZAPOTEC

PACIFIC

OCEAN

GULF O

▲ Pre-Classic Sites (2000 B.C.- 1 A.D.)
● Classic Sites (1 A.D.- 900 A.D.)
■ Post-Classic Sites (900 A.D.- 1520 A.D.)
◙ Classic-to-Post-Classic Sites
◈ Pre-Classic-to-Post-Classic Sites

REMNANTS OF THE PAST, the buildings and objects above are among the most notable creations of pre-Hispanic Mexico. The names in brown represent various important Mexican cultures, and are placed in the regions where each flourished. Smaller type indicates major archeological sites where remains have been found. At top is the Totonac Niche-Pyramid located at Tajín; other religious sites include the Pyramid of the Sun at Teotihuacán, the remains of the religious center at Monte Albán, the Temple of Kukulkan at Chichen Itzá,

never become known. The Spaniards, in their zeal both to subjugate and Christianize the New World, systematically set about destroying buildings, cities, works of art, pictographic records, everything they could find that was indicative of the level that the primitive Americans had achieved. What is known of ancient Mexico has been determined from fragments—the ruins of temples and cities (much of Mexico City is built of Aztec rubble), the telltale refuse strewn around age-old dwelling places or the occasional piece of sculpture or jewelry hidden in a grave, buried in dust or covered by jungle growth. The body of the knowledge is woefully incomplete and subject to constant revision and correction as new archeological sites are found and excavated. It is believed that Mexico contains at least 10,000 such sites still unexplored.

One of the earliest cultures, the so-called Olmec, flourished in the tropical lowlands of Veracruz where its traces are found in giant sculptured heads with moonlike faces and thick lips—a style that found its way into other early cultures of Mexico. In the Valley of Mexico, the Teotihuacán and Toltec cultures produced great ceremonial cities at San Juan Teotihuacán and at Tula. To the south, in the present state of Oaxaca, the Zapotecs and Mixtecs left traces of their greatness in the ruins of Monte Albán

Palenque's Temple of the Sun, and the fresco at Bonampák. Ceramic and stone figures are found along the coasts of the Gulf of Mexico and the Pacific. The Aztec statue of Coatlicue, a terrible death goddess, was found in the vicinity of the main square of today's Mexico City.

had in cotton, maguey and henequen), the early Mexicans lacked only two things that might have given their cultures permanence: beasts of burden and the wheel. All carrying was done on human backs. Under the circumstances this system may have been as efficient as any. The amount of commercial exchange between tribes was slight, and there were enough slaves to carry the burdens. The difficulties of the terrain had much to do with discouraging interchange. Had the country been more easily traversed, had it been more susceptible to the construction of roads, the old cultures might have survived and continued to advance, despite famine, depletion of the soil and other calamities. This of course would have made for interesting changes in the history of both the New World and the Old.

THE Mexicas or Aztecs, as they are more commonly known, were latecomers. They had been preceded in the Valley of Mexico by the builders of Teotihuacán and by the Toltecs. In response to a long-prophesied omen, the Aztecs in 1325 A.D. began to build the wondrous city of Tenochtitlán on an outcrop in the saline lake where Mexico City now stands. The omen: an eagle perched on a nopal cactus devouring a snake (the Mexican national emblem today). Using adobe bricks and elaborately carved stone with cedar and oak from the surrounding mountain slopes, they built a city that two centuries later caused the Spanish invaders to gasp in astonishment and admiration. Canals laced the island city. Great causeways connected it with the mainland. Aqueducts brought water from the springs of Chapultepec. Large temples and pyramids surrounded broad plazas. The markets were spotlessly clean and flowers cascaded from roof gardens.

For the Aztecs it was an excellent location. The climate was mild. The soil was fertile. The mountainsides were cloaked with trees whose roots helped to hold the runoff from the area's seasonal rains, giving the city a water supply from never-failing springs.

Even though communication was difficult, the Aztecs built up and maintained a primitive

and Mitla. To the east and farther southward are the ruins of the various Mayan civilizations. The architecture in all cases is startlingly evocative of modern design in its arrangement of mass, space and form, whether built with stone or adobe, with or without mortar, with peaked arches or flat roofs. Everywhere there is evidence of a highly developed aesthetic sense, in stone sculpture, ceramic work, the casting of precious metals, mosaics, the carving of crystal and jade—all achieved without metal tools.

With all these refinements, plus a staple crop that could be stored for the nonproductive months (a requisite of a settled versus nomadic existence) and fibers for weaving (which they but astonishingly effective network of commercial interchange and intelligence in the broad, loosely held dominion they established in central Mexico. Their religion demanded continual human sacrifices, and the need for sacrificial victims was met through conquest of other tribes. As tributaries, they were made to supply human victims as well as food, textiles and treasures for the Aztec storehouses. Broad plains to the north and passes through the mountains to the east, south and west provided workable access to all sections of the Aztec realm. Porters regularly brought fresh supplies of seafood from the Gulf Coast and rare fruits and vegetables, spices, aromatic woods and exotic flowers from the tropics for the pleasure of the Aztec priests and nobles.

TRAVELING merchants and traders doubled as espionage agents and reported all matters of consequence—a restlessness among a tributary people, a dangerous alliance, natural phenomena for the Aztec priests to ponder. Artists skilled at pictographic writing and portraiture were stationed in remote areas. Anything of interest was immediately recorded on cloth or bark paper and entrusted to relays of messengers who could be counted on to carry the news to Tenochtitlán with great speed.

This system of intelligence kept the Aztecs—by then the dominant people of Mexico—well-informed on the approaches of the Spaniards to the New World in the second decade of the 16th Century. Spain, then approaching the peak of empire, was eager for new land and new wealth. The ceaseless search for a passage to the Indies brought the Spaniards to continental North America. Soon after the first Spanish vessels, commanded by Hernández de Córdoba, skirted the coast of Mexico in February 1517, the Aztecs were hearing of "houses that move on water," as sailing ships were described. The visit of Juan de Grijalva the following year was recorded in greater detail. Thus the arrival of Hernán Cortés and his men in 1519 came as no surprise to the Aztecs. The Spaniards' every movement was recorded; their use of horses and

gunpowder was described to the Aztec rulers long before they actually saw either.

After the Conquest of Mexico by Cortés and his followers (see Chapter 3), the Spaniards built their colonial capital, which was to become Mexico City, on the ruins of Tenochtitlán, a city whose splendor had inspired one of the conquerors, Bernal Díaz del Castillo, to write that "never in the world would lands like these be discovered again." The location, an ideal one for the Aztecs, was a somewhat less happy choice for the Spaniards. The soil's fertility was easily exhausted. Construction of the city meant destruction of the forests for timber, and with the forests went the mountain springs and the dependable supply of water. Drainage was—and is—a problem in the old lake bed, surrounded as it is by high mountains. The Spaniards benefited from the prestige of occupying the Aztec capital city, but they paid for it with trouble and inconvenience. The city's limited accessibility had been no drawback to the Aztecs; from a defensive standpoint it had its virtues. Footpaths provided everything that was needed. But for the Spaniards, with their horses, mules and oxen, carts and wagons, roads had to be carved through the wild landscape.

THE pre-Hispanic system of communication and transportation was little improved in the three centuries of Spanish colonial rule. The Spaniards built roads only when they could contribute to the Spanish crown's principal interest in its vast new colony: the accumulation of wealth. Thus, roads were built to Pacific Coast ports to receive cargo from the Far East; to Veracruz on the Gulf for transshipment to Spain; and from the principal silver mines to the capital. Almost nothing was done to consolidate the vast territories of New Spain into anything like a homogeneous whole. The roads that had bound the Roman Empire together were almost totally lacking in the Spanish Empire. Aside from the cities the only outposts of Spanish rule were the haciendas and the religious missions which, if they survived, had to become self-sufficient and virtually independent small pockets of civilization in an otherwise empty land.

This heritage has persisted in Mexico until comparatively recent times. Roads were almost totally lacking in 19th Century Mexico. Political upheavals precluded any steps to unify the country. When, in the last quarter of the century, railroads began to be built, they were, for the most part, built by foreign concessionaires who planned them largely for the benefit of foreign trade, not for the unification of Mexico. The Mexican Revolution, when it was not conducted on foot or horseback, was fought on railroad cars. Railroads and even airplanes were to come to some remote parts of Mexico before highways would. Many a Mexican even today has ridden in an airplane before he has set his bare foot for the first time on a paved highway.

AS late as 1925 Mexico had only a few miles of improved roads, most of them connecting the capital with the nearby cities of Puebla and Toluca. By 1930 there were 885 miles of roads. In 1940 the total had reached more than 6,000 miles, by 1950 almost 16,000, by 1965 almost 39,500. Much of it was road building of the most difficult and expensive variety—the new highways snaking up and down mountains, creeping around precipices, bridging dizzy chasms, crossing bottomless swamps and turbulent rivers.

Good roads now span the length of the country, from the U.S. to the Guatemalan border. Yucatán, most remote of the Mexican states, has recently been connected with the rest of the country by highway. New highways are crossing the Sierras, reaching down from the central highlands to the lovely, isolated tropical towns of the Mexican coast. Where the roads go, schools are built, commerce grows, and fewer and fewer blank spots remain on the map of Mexico. Some of these isolated localities are still served by *arrieros*, the colorful drivers of strings of mules. These freighters of the back country with their cargoes of salt, tinware, gunpowder and nails—and sometimes a newspaper or a book—serve for many Mexicans as the only contact with the outside world.

Some areas, of course, do not even have the *arrieros*. Communities of indigenes such as the Lacandónes of the Chiapas jungle and the Seris on Tiburón Island in the Gulf of California survive in almost total isolation from the outside world. Little changed since pre-Conquest times, these people practice their own primitive agriculture, worship pre-Christian gods, follow the ancient crafts and many still fail to understand either the Spanish language or the meaning of modern Mexico.

In the mid-1930s, a quarter of a century after the overthrow of the dictator Porfirio Díaz and the beginning of the Mexican Revolution (and 20 years after Díaz' death in exile in Paris), an economist from Mexico City spent his vacation on a pack trip through the wild, cruelly beautiful sierra of Oaxaca, a remote country of jagged, vertical mountains and isolated valleys. He spent long days climbing range after range of peaks. In one lonely village, a mountain patriarch greeted him with great courtesy and dignity. Having done some wandering in his youth, the old man was the one person in the village who spoke Spanish. He provided hay and water for the horse and *tortillas*, beans and coffee for the traveler, and asked for news of the capital. The economist tried to give a simple summary of things that were happening in Mexico and the world. The patriarch listened carefully, brow knitted. Finally he asked: "And Don Porfirio, our president. Does he still have good health?"

BRINGING together this community and hundreds like it, scattered like fragments through the length and breadth of the rugged, forbidding land, is one of the most compelling tasks of Mexico's Revolution. To reach all the disparate inhabitants and to integrate them as functioning parts of the nation, to educate their children and bring their produce to the market place, to give them political responsibility—all this means conquering a landscape that is, at once, captivating and formidable.

RICH RESORT, Acapulco (*left*) was a merchant port for centuries. Today its lavish night clubs and luxury hotels draw thousands of visitors yearly.

BLEAK ROAD from Monterrey to Saltillo (*right*) passes the Sierra Madre foothills to link isolated communities with capital highways to Mexico City.

Roads To Bind a Split Nation

The city and country in Mexico seldom intermingle. A peasant who comes down from his mountain village to a sophisticated resort like Acapulco is a bewildered foreigner in the midst of his own countrymen. Between the city and his adobe hut lies a gulf of miles and centuries of isolation. Hundreds of villages remain remote, self-sufficient and starved of contact with life beyond the mountain rim. But today the immense gaps are slowly being spanned. In addition to the new trunk highways, miles of connecting roads now penetrate hitherto isolated rural areas.

MOUNTAIN FOLK of the central hills pursue an ancient way of life punctuated by the rare visits of a solitary priest

ARRIVING IN A VILLAGE, Father Enrique Salazar (*right*) passes a rural church. The 35 villages in his 900-square-mile parish are linked in some places only by mule paths.

VISITING A HUT in Tzicatlan, the padre comforts the mother of a stricken baby (*opposite*). He carries a stock of medicines, for there are no doctors in the region.

ASSEMBLING BY THE CHURCH, Otatitlan villagers (*below*) chat with Father Salazar (*second from right*). In these remote areas, the priest serves also as village counselor.

VILLAGE CONGREGATION in Tzicatlan watches as Father Salazar says Mass. The peasants are deeply religious, though frequently suspicious of Church officials.

MALARIA VICTIM, a young Tzicatlan girl (*right*) is blessed by Father Salazar as her husband watches. Tuberculosis and dysentery are also widespread in the area.

QUIET CONFESSION in a village church is made to the priest by a bridegroom before his marriage. Many of the churches consist of a single room, with no confessionals.

3

The Bitter
Heritage
of Conquest

DO not eat the first fruit of the year, one
is cautioned in rural Mexico, for it is
nourished with human blood. The Mexican
earth is rare that has not, at some time, been
soaked with the blood of Mexican fighting
foreigner or Mexican fighting Mexican.

More often than not the strife was inconclusive. The battle or war or revolution would
be fought again another day with a different
cast of characters. Indians fought for their
land at the time of the Conquest in the 16th
Century, fought for it in various uprisings
against the Spaniards and were still fighting
for it in the Revolution of the 20th Century.

The Church was embroiled in the War of Independence: the Virgin of Los Remedios was
named a general in the royalist forces to op-
pose the Virgin of Guadalupe, whose banner
was carried by Hidalgo's followers. It was still
embroiled during the *Cristero* uprisings of the
1920s. Mexicans have fought invaders from
Spain, France and the United States—but most
often they have fought Mexicans. The old issues were never wholly resolved, and the old
hatreds have had a way of enduring.

Nowhere is this better shown than in Mexican attitudes toward Hernán Cortés, who sub-
jugated the country early in the 16th Century

39

and had more to do with shaping its history and destiny, for better or worse, than any other individual. Today, four and one half centuries after the Conquest, attitudes toward Cortés are still a divisive element in Mexico. There is not a single monument to Cortés in the entire republic. This is not because Cortés' memory is one of unmitigated villainy. Killer, destroyer and gold-mad intriguer though he may have been, Cortés was, by comparison with other swashbuckling adventurers of his day, a humane and enlightened man, a developer as well as a looter, a friend, ultimately, of the Indians he had quelled and a man of conscience—which the greater number of his fellow conquerors were not. But the memory of Cortés in Mexico remains one of violence, cruelty, foreign intervention, colonialism, imposition and repression.

IN 1946 a little party of scholars and historians, armed with hammers, chisels and an age-yellowed document, opened up a wall in the old chapel of the Hospital of Jesus in Mexico City. The chapel had been closed for at least 20 years. Gold leaf flaked from the old altar and pigeons fluttered in the dusty air. Behind a stone slab in the wall the searchers found what they were looking for: a velvet-covered casket enclosing a glass urn. Within the urn, tied up in a cambric scarf and black ribbons, were the mortal remains of Hernán Cortés—a skull and a clutch of bones—along with a notarized document. Almost four centuries had passed since the conqueror had died in Spain, and this was the seventh resting place for his remains—a secret one. In 1823 when the remains of heroes of the War of Independence had been ceremoniously reinterred in Mexico City it had been felt that there might be riots at the most recent grave of Cortés. The bones had been removed to the secret, unmarked place in the wall of a chapel that Cortés himself, centuries earlier, had ordered built.

In due course the remains of Cortés were quietly placed back in the church wall and sealed, but by then the discovery had set off a great public outcry and a battle of symbols: on the one side Cortés, and on the other the last of the Aztec rulers, Cuauhtémoc. Ultranationalist researchers claimed to have found evidence that Cortés was not the well set-up, somberly handsome man he had been pictured as in the past (even by his contemporary critics), but was instead an ugly, misshapen, bandy-legged, runtish creature, and this corrected version was forthwith incorporated in a mural by the painter Diego Rivera. At the same time the memory of Cuauhtémoc was reinforced by the discovery of what was described as *his* burial place in a remote village in the state of Guerrero, hundreds of miles from the place of his death in the jungles of southern Mexico. Scholars viewed the latter discovery *con mucho ojo* (with much eye), an expression of doubt which can be reduced to a hand gesture: the thumb and forefinger holding the lids of one eye far apart. But this did not deny the fact that Cuauhtémoc, the Indian hero, represented everything that Cortés was not: a martyr in Mexico's never-ending struggle to recapture, keep and maintain its independence.

AS in all symbolism and generalization the facts tended to become a little hazy. Cortés was not all villain, and the Aztecs were far from the noblest aborigines of pre-Conquest Mexico. They were, instead, regarded with as much hatred and fear by the other Indians as would be the Spaniards. Warlike, tough, domineering and driven by a harsh, demanding religion, they had pushed the boundaries of their area of influence as far as the Pánuco River on the north and into Central America on the south. They regularly exacted heavy tribute from the peoples they had overcome—gold, silver, precious stones, food, clothing and, most important, sacrificial victims by the hundreds and thousands to be immolated on the pyramids of Tenochtitlán.

The Aztecs in the early 16th Century were less than 200 years old as an established, settled nation; their accomplishments in city building and in the arts and sciences, while impressive, were not unprecedented in the rich cultures of ancient Mexico. Their greatest deeds had been in the field of war and conquest. Without the profound hatred that this engendered, it is doubtful that Cortés and his little band of freebooters could have maintained a beachhead in the New World. As it was, unhappy victims of the Aztecs directed the Spaniards' footsteps toward Tenochtitlán and even furnished Indian warriors and porters by the thousands to speed them on their way.

When Juan de Grijalva, one of Cortés' precursors, went ashore in 1518 in what is now the state of Tabasco, there were parleys and an exchange of trinkets with the local Indians. The natives were apologetic about the paucity of their gold, but they did say that if it was gold the white man wanted, he could get plenty of it by going inland to the Aztecs' capital. The Indians sensed that the white man's eagerness for gold meant trouble. No one deserved it any more than the Aztecs, and anyway they had all the gold.

Grijalva did not take the hint. But Cortés, when he followed Grijalva west the next year, was to hear the same words again, and—wily, imaginative and resourceful man that he was—he picked up the clue.

A little later he landed near what is now Veracruz and was met by emissaries from Moctezuma, the powerful Aztec ruler, who had been informed about the white men and their leader, and their eagerness for gold. The emissaries presented gifts to Cortés of fine cloth, feather mosaic work, precious stones and quantities of gold and silver. Albrecht Dürer, the great German artist, saw some of these treasures in Europe in 1520 and observed: "I saw the things that were brought to the King from the New Golden Land: a sun entirely of gold, a whole fathom broad; like-

wise a moon, entirely of silver, just as large; likewise sundry curiosities. . . . These things were all so precious that they were valued at a hundred thousand gulden worth. But I have never seen in all my days what so rejoiced my heart as these things. For I saw among them amazing artistic objects, and I marveled over the subtle ingenuity of the men in these distant lands."

After making their presentations to Cortés, Moctezuma's emissaries asked him to leave. But Cortés asked for an appointment with Moctezuma and explained that the Spaniards suffered from an illness for which gold was the only specific. The emissaries went off to fetch more gold, and Cortés studied the situation.

The Totonac people of Cempoala, near Veracruz, were eager to tell him of the troubles they had as vassals of the Aztecs. They were ready to march with him against Tenochtitlán if he would accept them.

Cortés found additional allies among the Tlaxcalans, neighbors and enemies of the Aztecs. At first the Tlaxcalans fought the Spaniards fiercely, suspecting an Aztec trick. But when Cortés demonstrated that he had no alliance with the hated Aztecs and that the Spaniards were formidable fighters in their own right, the Tlaxcalans accepted them. It was the most important friendship Cortés was to make in all his adventures in the New World.

This, then, was the first of Mexico's many revolutions, containing most of the elements that were to repeat themselves in later eruptions: a hard-handed custodian of power and a huge, treacherous vacuum between the wealth and luxury of the overlords and the poverty of the subject peoples.

The quick-witted Cortés grasped the new alliance readily, and instead of the 500 Spanish adventurers who had come with him, he

MONTEZUMA, MOCTEZUMA

To Spaniards hearing the guttural Nahuatl language in the 16th Century, the name of the Aztec chief sounded like "Montezuma." This became the common usage—as it is in the U.S. Marine's hymn. But experts today agree that "Moctezuma" is closer to the original Nahuatl.

marched toward the Aztecs' Tenochtitlán with an array of almost 7,000 warriors and porters.

There were other things at work for him, too—shadowy figures from a mysterious past who live on in modern Mexico. One of these was a fascinating Indian woman, Doña Marina as the Spanish called her, or Malinche as the Indians said (she became so closely identified with Cortés in the Indian mind that after a time he too was known to them simply as Malinche). She had been given to the Spaniards as a going-away present at one of their early stops in Mexico. She had been born among a people who spoke Nahuatl, the language of the Aztecs, but as a child had been sold into slavery among the Mayas and thus knew both languages. Cortés had with him a Spanish cleric who had been shipwrecked among the Mayas some time before and could speak their language. Through the two of them Cortés had a linguistic bridge to the Aztecs and to other Nahuatl-speaking peoples, without which he could not have understood, let alone taken advantage of, the strange situation. Malinche in consequence was never far from his side, translating his speeches about the great Spanish king across the sea, the true religion and Cortés' fraternal intentions, and in turn explaining to him the response of the natives and their state of mind. At a somewhat later date she bore him a son, Martín Cortés, who many years afterward was to figure in an abortive uprising against the Spaniards his mother had helped.

Even more shadowy, but a figure of equal importance in the Conquest, was the legendary man-god or god-man Quetzalcoatl, who was variously identified as the feathered serpent god, as the god of the wind, of life, of twins

POTENT FORCE, the man-god Quetzalcoatl appears in an Indian drawing in one of his several manifestations.

and of monsters, as the planet Venus, as creator of man and as the great civilizer of ancient Mexico. The Quetzalcoatl cult was functioning in ancient America well before the Christian era in the Old World. Quetzalcoatl himself was thought of as a benign personage with a fair skin and a beard, who taught the arts of feather work, carving, cultivating maize, spinning and weaving cotton, and working with precious stones and metals. He was said to have created man by taking a bundle of old bones he had picked up in the underworld and sprinkling them with his own blood to give them life. He eschewed human sacrifice, incontinence and drunkenness. The code he prescribed was one of almost Christian asceticism.

The legend says that Quetzalcoatl was, finally, tricked into debauchery. Filled with shame, he fled, escaping on a raft made of serpent skins. He sailed toward the east, promising to return in the year of *Ce Acatl*, or One Reed. The year of One Reed in the Aztec calendar just happened to be 1519 in the Julian calendar— the year that Cortés arrived. Cortés and his men came from the east, the direction in which the legend said Quetzalcoatl had disappeared. And they were, as Quetzalcoatl had been, fair-skinned and bearded.

This series of remarkable coincidences was the undoing of Moctezuma, the Aztec ruler. A priest-king, he was much given to superstitious brooding, and he had been pondering a series of strange things—celestial phenomena, earth tremors and visions—when word reached him of the Spaniards' arrival. Moctezuma's attitude toward the advancing Spaniards went through a series of quick, puzzling shifts— hospitality, deference, fear and confusion. It was suspected that the Spaniards might be gods

—a suspicion that Cortés did everything in his power to encourage.

When the Spaniards finally made their way into Tenochtitlán they were welcomed gravely by a tractable Moctezuma, who made them comfortable in his father's palace and showed them his city and all its wonders. When the prowling Spaniards uncovered a great cache of ancestral gold and jewels, Moctezuma told them to help themselves and ordered chieftains of tributary tribes to bring still more gold. He became a captive spokesman for the Spaniards and when, after eight months of occupation, his subjects rose in rebellion against the interlopers, he was stoned to death, possibly by his own people. The Spaniards were forced to beat a bloody retreat; so loaded were many of them with Aztec gold that when they fell from the causeways into the water they quickly sank. The event later came to be called *la noche triste*, the sad night.

The survivors of *la noche triste* retreated to Tlaxcala, reinforced themselves and again marched on Tenochtitlán, this time an armed and angry city. The Europeans and their Indian allies fought their way back in, inch by inch, destroying as they came, leveling the city, filling the noble streets and canals with Indian dead.

AFTER the death of Moctezuma, the Aztecs were led first by Cuitláhuac, Moctezuma's brother, who ruled for only 80 days before succumbing to smallpox (one of the deadliest weapons the Spaniards had imported), and then by the unyielding, resourceful Cuauhtémoc, Moctezuma's nephew and son-in-law, whose name, appropriately, meant fallen eagle. Although Moctezuma's name is better known abroad, that of Cuauhtémoc is more illustrious in Mexico itself.

Cuauhtémoc fiercely rejected all suggestions of surrender, but in the end, with all his people either killed in battle or near death from starvation, he was captured. He declared to Cortés: "I have done what I was obliged to do in the defense of my city and my people.

I can do no more. . . . Take that dagger from your belt and kill me with it, quickly."

Cortés passed up what might have been a humane solution to the Cuauhtémoc problem. The conqueror's followers, gold-hungry as always and bitterly disappointed that the ruined city had provided so little loot, tortured the prince by painting his feet with oil and thrusting them among live coals, in a vain effort to make him disclose the hiding place of the royal treasures.

Afterwards Cortés kept the long-suffering Cuauhtémoc as a hostage against an uprising of the remnants of the Aztec nation. Three years later, during an expedition to Honduras to quell a revolt among his own men, Cortés learned, he said, that the accompanying Indians were planning an uprising against the Spaniards. Cuauhtémoc was questioned. He conceded that the Indians had, from time to time, talked of an uprising, but that he himself had discouraged it. Cortés refused to believe him and ordered him hanged from a *ceiba* tree. Cuauhtémoc was bitter. "I knew what it was to trust your false promises, Malinche," he is quoted as saying. "I knew that you had destined me for this fate. . . . Why do you slay me so unjustly? God will demand it of you!" He had by this time apparently absorbed at least a smattering of the Christian religion, which the Spaniards had brought with them to the new land, and with a fine sense of irony threw it in the face of his tormentor.

THE emotions that beset the Conquest— greed, superstition, hatred and fear—live on in Mexico today, as does the cast of characters. Cuauhtémoc's execution assured that both he and his executioner would become symbols: the one of Indian Mexico's stoicism and courage, the other of the ruthless foreigner, the exploiter. Cuauhtémoc is honored in monuments, political speeches and names of streets and towns (and also in a first-rate brewery), and each year on the anniversary of his torture an Indian dancing fraternity performs traditional dances around his statue on Mexico City's Paseo de la Reforma.

There are no monuments to Malinche, Cortés' Indian mistress and interpreter. She was finally married off to one of Cortés' lieutenants and faded away in history. But her name lives on in the Mexican vocabulary. A *malinchista* is one who sells out country or friends, who consorts with foreigners and bestows favors on them at the expense of his countrymen. *Malinchismo* ranks high among the misdeeds for which Mexicans condemn one another. Malinche has also become a prominent ghost, the spirit of a sad woman who rides the night wind, a dweller in caves whose weeping voice the imaginative often hear at night in the sound of the rain and the wind.

THE three centuries of Mexico's existence as a Spanish colony were a period of tranquillity, almost of stagnation. Spain was less interested in building a functioning empire than in establishing a source of steady income. Within 25 years of the Conquest the boundaries of New Spain, as the colony was called, had been pushed far into California, around the Gulf of Mexico to the northeast and almost to Panama on the south. But the geographical expansion was consolidated only where there was a prospect of quick wealth. If there were mines or rich farming land, tight control was established; if not, the conquerors were content to mark the area as Spanish territory on the maps, send in missionary priests and a few soldiers, and let it go at that.

New Spain was actually a disappointment to the new overlords. The abundance of gold and jewels that had been concentrated in the hands of the Aztecs was deceptive. During several centuries of exacting tribute from subject peoples the Aztecs had accumulated an impressive hoard. More impressed with aesthetic than intrinsic values, the Aztecs gave gold freely to their conquerors, and the latter assumed that the country abounded in it. They discovered, to their sorrow, that there was very little of it. There was silver (and in the course of three centuries of colonialism Spain took more than $2 billion from its colony, the bulk of it in bullion and minted silver). There was agricultural wealth to be had, but it required, as did mining, tremendous amounts of manual labor. In due course the Spaniards discovered that Mexico's greatest natural resource was really the Indian. Indian labor could convert the country's less obvious resources into something of value.

RECOGNITION by the Spaniards of the vital role of the Indians in producing wealth led, ironically, to the survival of these native peoples in Mexico. This was in dramatic contrast to the situation in the English colonies in North America, where the red men were regarded as nothing more than a nuisance and were therefore reduced to insignificant numbers. But if the Indians survived in Mexico it was at a bare subsistence level. The *encomienda* system, which had already been used in the Spanish West Indian colonies, was brought into Mexico and put into full play. Soldiers of the Conquest were rewarded with grants of land and *encomiendas* of Indians. A deed of *encomienda* or entrustment read: "Unto you are given in trust [number] Indians for you to make use of in your farms and mines; and you are to teach them the things of the holy Catholic faith."

Such grants were outwardly for the purpose of safeguarding, protecting and Christianizing the natives. Actually they were grants of free labor. If the Indians rebelled or attempted escape, they were literally branded as slaves and treated as such (even infants in arms could be regarded as rebels and thus branded). For the Indians the end result was largely the same. Slavery under any circumstances was eventually outlawed, and so, in time, was the *encomienda* system. But by that time the Indians were tied to hacienda or mine by debt, and their lot was little improved.

Spain's record was not all black, however. Of the 63 viceroys who represented the Spanish throne during the colonial era, a number made solid contributions to the development of the country. One was Antonio de Mendoza, who opened a college for Indian youth and also established the New World's first printing press. Another was Luis de Velasco, who in 1553 inaugurated what was to become the National University—the first institution of higher education on the North American continent—and who consistently took the side of the Indians in the never-ending disputes with the holders of *encomiendas*.

Although it was not quite accurate to say, as King Ferdinand VI of Spain did some time later, that "the preaching of the gospel, the uprooting of idolatry and the drawing of the Indians from the darkness and error in which they live" had been the "principal motive" of the Conquest, the most benevolent face that Spain exhibited in the New World was that of the Catholic Church. Priests accompanied the conquerors and in some cases managed to curb their excesses. The conquerors were followed by missionary priests from Spain: first the Franciscans, later the Dominicans, the Augustinians and the Jesuits. The first two orders pioneered in the most remote areas and invariably assumed, as one of their prime responsibilities, the protection of the Indians from the greed and cruelty of the *encomenderos*.

THE friars learned the Indian languages and quickly gained the trust and affection of the Indians. One of them, Bartolomé de las Casas, a strong-minded, argumentative Dominican who had served as a missionary in the West Indies and later became Bishop of Chiapas in Mexico, took the radical position that Indians not only were human but also had souls. He was hated by the Spaniards in Mexico and his views were widely circulated by Spain's enemies in Europe. A Franciscan friar, Bernardino de Sahagún, unlike the priests who systematically tried to destroy all traces of Indian culture, studied and carefully preserved, in both the Nahuatl tongue and Spanish, as much as could be salvaged of the history, folklore and religious beliefs of the Aztecs. Vasco de

Quiroga, Bishop of Michoacán, established schools and built up native crafts and industry —gold and silver work, painting, wood carving, pottery and weaving; he was known, and still is affectionately referred to, not as Bishop Quiroga but as Tata Vasco, or Daddy Vasco.

Other missionaries introduced the Indians to wheeled vehicles, draft animals, iron tools such as plows, shovels, hoes and axes, the raising of livestock and poultry, and more efficient methods of spinning, weaving, dyeing and pottery making. The addition of European ideas and techniques to the natives' talent for work in wood and stone and decorative materials resulted in colonial buildings that, in their intricate beauty, were an improvement on their sources, Spanish and Indian alike.

BUT despite the efforts of the friars, Spain had no intention of allowing its New World colony to become anything other than a captive market and a supplier of wealth (by the beginning of the 19th Century New Spain alone was providing almost two thirds of Spain's revenues). The Indians were not only prevented from making or carrying arms and from riding horses—and discouraged from trying to learn the Spanish language; they were also forbidden to engage in the jewelry craft or to work with their own cochineal dye— which Europe had not known of before the discovery of Mexico. It was against colonial law for residents of New Spain to cultivate grapes and olives or to deal in salt, tobacco, playing cards or even in ice brought from snow-capped volcanoes. All of these undertakings were classified as royal monopolies.

Trade with other countries—even with fellow Spanish colonies—was forbidden, and what trade there was had to move in Spanish ships; if there were no Spanish ships, trade stood still. Mexican raw materials—metals, fibers, dyestuffs—were exported to Spain, but since Spain did little or no manufacturing these were in turn shipped to other European countries. Finished goods were then sold to Spain, and Spain thereupon sold them to the colony at prices that had, by this time, become enormously swollen.

New Spain was not permitted to develop any degree of economic independence. Nor were the inhabitants given any opportunity to acquire experience in self-government. Insofar as New Spain was governed locally, it was ruled by Spanish emigrés called *gachupines*, wearers of spurs. Between the *gachupines* and the Creoles—Spaniards born in the colony—there was a great social and official gulf. Creoles were regarded as inferior and were excluded from positions of importance and responsibility. Many of them were nevertheless wealthy and led lives of arrogant indolence. The more serious ones, the intellectuals, formed a restless nucleus around which the independence movement would later grow. The mestizos or mixed bloods—Spanish-Indian, Spanish-Negro and Indian-Negro—occupied correspondingly lower strata in the caste system, while the pure-blooded Indians, who comprised almost half the population, were the lowest of all.

"As long as there is a cobbler from Castile or a mule from La Mancha," said one of New Spain's governing officials, "to them will belong the government of America." And in 1767—a time when the ferment of freedom was beginning to stir in other parts of the world—a Spanish viceroy advised his subjects in New Spain: "For once and all, know that you have been born to be silent and to obey, and neither to discuss nor hold opinions upon the exalted affairs of the government."

THERE were flurries of revolt all through the three centuries of colonialism. The Mixtón war in 1541—a rising of Chichimec Indians in western Mexico—temporarily threatened Spanish rule. The Mayan Indians of Yucatán fiercely resisted the Spaniards from the outset and were among the last of the native peoples to be subdued. Three of Cortés' sons, one of them legitimate, were involved in an abortive Creole plot in 1565-1566; there were scattered risings by Indians, mestizos and Negroes, mutinies by miners and tobacco workers, and riots

during the periodic famines. But these revolts were ineffectual.

It was not until early in the 19th Century that a really serious threat was made against Spanish rule, and this came at a time when Spain as a governing entity had almost disappeared. From its high tide of empire in the 16th Century, Spain had gone steadily downhill, its power and authority dwindling. Charles IV, a weak-willed king, abdicated in 1808 in favor of his son, Ferdinand VII. During a visit to Spain's supposed ally, France, they were both imprisoned. Joseph Bonaparte, brother of France's Napoleon, was placed on the throne of Spain. Popular juntas, liberal in tone, were the only surviving elements of Spanish sovereignty. In Mexico this led to an ironic situation. The *gachupines*, rigidly conservative in their outlook, maintained a loyalty to the liberal Spanish juntas, which they thought offered the best chance of preserving the link between Mexico and Spain. But the Creoles, who had been influenced by some of the liberalism abroad in the world thanks to the anti-royalist American and French revolutions, hated the *gachupines* and maintained their allegiance to the throneless Spanish king, Ferdinand.

THE Creoles were unable to unite, but some of them did become leaders in the struggle to free Mexico. The man who was later to be recognized as the father of Mexican independence was a Creole named Miguel Hidalgo y Costilla, an elderly, kindhearted, bookish parish priest of the town of Dolores in west central Mexico, who had absorbed some ideas of liberty and the rights of man. Father Hidalgo had given expression to his own rebelliousness by encouraging his Indian parishioners to plant vineyards and olive and mulberry trees in defiance of colonial law. He had encouraged them to develop pottery and leatherworking enterprises, had taught them Spanish, had organized a town band and was loved by his parishioners.

Hidalgo belonged to a liberal discussion group, one of several in the country by this time, which talked of an independent Mexico ruled by Ferdinand VII. Their vague conspiracy was discovered, however, and Hidalgo, with little planning and no very clear notion of his aims, summoned his parishioners to church on September 16, 1810, and gave his *grito* (cry) of liberty: "Mexicans! *Viva* Mexico, *viva* Independence, *viva* the Virgin of Guadalupe!" His listeners echoed his *vivas* and grimly added: "Death to the *gachupines*!"

With this as a battle cry—one that is repeated in every town in Mexico on the eve of each September 16—Hidalgo and his followers, carrying a banner of the Virgin of Guadalupe and armed with sticks, stones, knives, axes and machetes, set off to liberate Mexico. They were wholly unschooled in and unprepared for military operations. Some of Hidalgo's men later were to try to stop royalist artillery by holding their straw sombreros over the mouths of cannon. But Indians and mestizos alike deserted mines and haciendas to join them. Small ranchers, mule drivers, bandits and guerrilla units led by other village priests joined the mob.

As news of the movement spread, there were other risings in northern and western Mexico. Hidalgo's aims were modest enough: he wanted a congress which would govern Mexico in the name of Ferdinand, and he proclaimed the abolition of Indian tribute and the restoration to the Indians of their historic lands. But his rebellion soon grew into a much more extensive and violent affair. His army marched through town after town. In Guanajuato the garrison and the *gachupines* barricaded themselves in a grain warehouse. They were overcome by the suicidal attack of Hidalgo's primitive army and massacred; their town was looted.

HIDALGO'S Creole associates were alienated by the haphazard air of the uprising, but the rebel forces grew to 80,000. They drove through city after city, arriving finally almost on the outskirts of the capital, where they soundly defeated the defending royalist forces. But then they failed to follow their advantage and, instead, withdrew. The rebellion disintegrated. Hidalgo was excommunicated by his church, betrayed, captured by the royalists and executed. His head and those of other rebels were placed in cages on the warehouse walls of Guanajuato, the scene of their first victory.

After his execution his captors exhibited what they described as Hidalgo's retraction. The document declared that Mexico was not yet prepared for independence. Of this there could be little doubt. Prepared or not, however, Father Hidalgo's revolution had demonstrated clearly the Mexicans' explosive desire for freedom. It was a desire that was to smoulder for another century—even after independence from Spain—occasionally bursting into flames, before the outbreak of the revolution that was to make the Mexicans truly free.

THE struggle begun by Father Hidalgo was carried on by one of his followers, also a priest, José María Morelos y Pavón. A mestizo, Morelos was a shrewder military commander than Hidalgo and a man of clearer objectives. Had he pressed his military advantages Mexican independence might have been achieved earlier and much turmoil averted. But Morelos interrupted the fighting to assemble a congress and proclaim the Republic of Anáhuac (after the old Indian name for the plateau on which Mexico City lies). He proposed to confiscate the wealth of rich individuals and of the Church and to divide it between the government and the poor. He also aimed to restore lands to dispossessed peasants and to abolish the special privileges of the military and clergy. His preoccupation with such matters led to his defeat and execution, the second martyr of the struggle for independence. The policies which he enunciated, however, formed a foundation for all the revolutionary movements to come.

Mexican independence was finally achieved in 1821 (see Chapter 4). It came not so much through Mexican victory as through Spanish inability to control the New World colonies. But, far from bringing peace, Mexico's independence initiated a century of struggle and bloodshed, and it was only at the end of that period that modern Mexico emerged.

A Nation's Past Revived and Revered

When the Spaniards came to Mexico in the early 16th Century they did their best to obliterate a magnificent Indian culture. Today archeologists are methodically recovering Mexico's once-forgotten past. Dozens of Mayan religious centers have been freed of smothering jungle. Diggers sifting the debris of centuries have laid bare a score of ancient cities. Amid the ruins of Monte Albán, Chichén Itzá and San Juan Teotihuacán, teams of scholars have reconstructed the work of long-dead architects. At hundreds of sites the triumphs of once-thriving civilizations now obtrude sharply from the Mexican terrain.

EMERGING from the jungle floor, an Olmecan stone face (*opposite*) almost 3,000 years old bakes in a tropic sun.

Gleaming white in the hot Mexican sun, a group of Mayan residential buildings, part of the remains of the Indian city of Uxmal, lie

abandoned in the hills of northern Yucatán. The well-preserved structures, set in a quadrangle, probably served as priests' quarters.

COBBLED STREET winds by colonial stucco houses (*opposite*) in Guanajuato. Spaniards laid out entire towns according to Renaissance design theories.

YOUNG FLOCK files out of a chapel near Mexico City after Palm Sunday Mass. The zeal of Spanish priests has left Mexico 95 per cent Catholic.

Moving along briskly, revolutionary forces led by the guerrilla chiefs Emiliano Zapata (center, in ornamented coat) and Pancho Villa

(right, wearing military uniform) take Mexico City in 1914.

4

The Delayed Revolution

FOR the visitor who questions the headlong impetuosity with which Mexico today is plunging ahead with unorthodox programs of industrialization, public works and social welfare, Mexican officials have a stock answer. They are trying, they explain, to compress into a few decades what other countries have managed to spread over a century or more. Mexico, they continue, managed to misplace a century—the years between the War for Independence and the Revolution.

The men who offer this explanation and who are guiding the destinies of Mexico today are for the most part the second or third generation of the Revolution. They are sober, dedicated and driven by a sense of great urgency. They are educated men—technicians, specialists, engineers, economists, industrialists, social scientists. They are loyal to the old revolutionary slogans, but they are more immediately concerned with things like population projections, productivity estimates and educational goals. They offer a sharp contrast to the colorful leaders and desperate fighters of their fathers' generation, and an even sharper one to the procession of ill-assorted characters who dominated Mexico in the 19th Century.

Mexico's independence, which dates officially from 1821, when the last of the Spanish viceroys acknowledged it, was not so much achieved by concerted action as it was gained almost by default. The dominant figure at the close of the colonial period in Mexico was Agustín de Iturbide, a royalist colonel who had defeated the Morelos forces in the field. But instead of preserving New Spain for the empire, Iturbide acquired his own ideas about independence and turned against the Spaniards. With Mexico free of Spanish rule, he had himself declared Emperor Agustín I of Mexico. "You know how to be free," he told his people. "You must now learn to be happy." After a year of pomp and pageantry he ran out of funds, was ousted and went into exile. But the deed was done: for better or for worse, Mexico was finally its own master.

M ORE sinister was Antonio López de Santa Anna, an erratic military genius of gloomy countenance who described himself as the Napoleon of the West. Santa Anna was to rule Mexico 11 separate times between 1833 and 1855. His political affiliations swung from liberal (he was involved in the ouster of Iturbide) to clerical-conservative. He is remembered in Mexico as the author of disaster. When the Texas colonists in 1835-1836 rebelled against Mexico—fighting, at first, not for independence but only for a return to constitutional guarantees—Santa Anna set in motion a dolorous chain of events. He marched into Texas, besieged the Alamo and slaughtered the survivors of the siege. After bringing about another massacre at Goliad, he finally met defeat at the hands of the Texans under Sam Houston at San Jacinto. He offered to trade Texas its independence for his personal freedom.

The separation of Texas led a decade later to war with the United States. Mexico not only lost its last claim to Texas, but gave up California and other northern areas, a loss of 918,-355 square miles of territory in all, more than half of the nation's prewar area. The loss was made more grievous by the discovery, almost immediately afterward, of gold in California. A little later, back in power for the 11th time, Santa Anna was pressed for cash to pay the troops that upheld his regime. He sold the Mesilla Valley, now a part of Arizona and New Mexico, to the United States for $10 million. In 18 years Mexico was reduced from a position of territorial pre-eminence—comparable to that of Russia, China or Brazil—to one of relative insignificance. This was due partly to the past failure of Spain to consolidate its geographical holdings, partly to the burgeoning ambitions of the United States, but largely to the recklessness of Santa Anna.

F ROM the beginning of Mexico's existence as an independent nation, there was a constant seesaw between liberals and conservatives —the ideological heirs of Hidalgo and Morelos on one side, the landowners, clergy and aristocracy on the other. The most prominent of the liberal figures to emerge—and one of the most revered men in Mexican history—was Benito Juárez, a Zapotec Indian, ascetic and of dour mien, with an almost mystical regard for law. Juárez was the author of some of the reform measures that went into the new constitution of 1857, which, among other things, forbade the Church to own real estate, abolished special privileges of the military and clergy, called for free education and freedom of the press and assembly, and permitted priests and nuns to renounce their vows. The constitution was not only bitterly resisted by the Mexican conservatives, but even brought a condemnation from Pope Pius IX. " . . . [it] allows the free exercise of all cults," said the Pope, "and admits the right of pronouncing in public every kind of thought and opinion. . . . [We] declare null and void the said decrees."

When the incumbent president failed to enforce the law, the legislature declared his office vacant, and Juárez, as chief justice, was elevated to the presidency. The country was plunged into the three-year (1857-1860) civil strife called the War of the Reform, a fierce, bloody struggle marked by excesses on both sides. At the war's conclusion, Juárez took over the administration of a country that was on the verge of ruin and bankruptcy. The inability of Mexico to meet its foreign debt payments led to intervention, first by France, Spain and England jointly, and later by France alone. Mexican conservatives had, meanwhile, conspired with France's ambitious Napoleon III to put an unemployed Austrian archduke, Maximilian, on the "imperial" throne of Mexico.

The blond-bearded Maximilian was a well-meaning man whose liberal instincts brought consternation to his rightist backers. He assumed the throne after being assured by the French that he had been "elected" by the Mexicans. He was more interested in botanizing, butterfly collecting and compiling a manual of court etiquette than in ruling. When the French forces withdrew, his regime crumbled. He was shot in 1867 by a Juarist firing squad.

Juárez, once more able to function as president, initiated fiscal reforms to rescue Mexico from bankruptcy, helped foster the development of industry and transportation and started building a system of free public education. A plain, honest, stubborn man, he began the molding of modern Mexico. When he died in office in 1872, Mexico had become a nation, half a century after it had ceased being a colony.

ONE of Juárez' generals, Porfirio Díaz, was to rule Mexico longer than any man in history—from 1876 to 1910. There was a four-year interval in which Díaz put a puppet in the presidential chair because of the law against re-election; after that he merely changed the law. Díaz was a mestizo from Oaxaca. Like Juárez, he loved his country and had great aspirations for it. But unlike his predecessor he was wildly ambitious, given to ostentation and pomp, ruthless in achieving his ends and oblivious to legal and moral strictures. Where

Juárez built up from the soil and the constitution, erecting schools and respecting the rights of others, Díaz wanted to impose improvement from the top down. He felt this was the only hope for the Mexican people, who, he insisted, had demonstrated no ability either to govern or to improve themselves.

Díaz' name lives on in the language. *Porfirista* is used to describe archconservative political, economic or social ideas, totalitarianism in government and turn-of-the-century ornateness in architecture and decoration. The most imposing relic of *porfirismo* in Mexico is Mexico City's ostentatious Palace of Fine Arts. Although it was not actually completed until long after the Díaz regime, it was conceived and begun then, and its most obvious characteristics are reminiscent of the grandeur Díaz sought, in his way, to bring to Mexico. It contains glass domes, heroic statuary, monumental columns, intricate stone carvings, stately porticoes, great halls, three kinds of marble and, in the auditorium, a gaudy glass curtain weighing 22 tons which was made to order by Tiffany of New York City.

MUCH that Díaz tried to do in Mexico coincides with what Mexico is trying to do today. He promoted the industrialization, modernization and political stabilization of a land that had suffered badly from primitivism and instability. It would seem, then, that the old man with the eagle-wing mustaches would be revered in modern Mexico. He rarely is. The Porfirian Peace, as his long period of control was known, was maintained, as they said, through the four P's—*pan o palo, plata o plomo,* bread or club, silver or lead. It was a period in which a few people acquired great wealth, while the rest of Mexico was poorer than ever.

Díaz ruthlessly suppressed objections to his methods, halting any expression of critical opinion. The press was throttled. Troublesome journalists were often jailed, sometimes killed. The legislature consisted of a list of names that Díaz would draw up and publish. One member of an important family was given a

The Delayed Revolution

state governorship because he had seduced his niece and it was felt that a position of responsibility might be a sobering influence.

Díaz made his peace with the Catholic Church, secretly promising that Juárez' reform laws would be overlooked in return for the right of approval of clerical appointments (a handy way to prevent the rise of another Hidalgo or Morelos). The Church again began to accumulate property. The President ended banditry by putting the bandits in uniform, creating a new police force, the *rurales*. In their tight-fitting uniforms and their wide hats, the pistol-happy *rurales*, alert to any restlessness, kept a close watch on the peasants, teaching and enforcing obsequiousness to the "decent people."

Public lands were offered for sale to favored persons at ridiculous prices. Ninety-six million acres, about one fifth of the total area of the nation, were sold to 17 such persons: four of them got more than 25 million acres in Lower California; another got 17 million acres in Chihuahua; another 12 million. The Indians were left with less land than they had had at any time in history.

IN the northwest the Yaqui Indians were driven into rebellion so that their ancestral communally held lands could be seized and converted into privately owned plantations. During the fighting, bounties were given to anyone who brought in a Yaqui ear or hand. Captive Yaquis were shipped to the chicle and henequen plantations in Quintana Roo and Yucatán, where they were sold at prices ranging from 25 to 75 pesos a head.

Attempts to organize labor were put down ruthlessly. When strikes were called at the Río Blanco textile mills and at the Cananea copper smelter, troops were sent in to shoot down the strikers and restore the Porfirian Peace.

Meanwhile Díaz was encouraging foreign investment in Mexico so as to build more railroads, dredge harbors, erect factories and search for oil. He rewarded such investors with lavish concessions, gifts of land and exemptions from Mexican laws and taxes. The inducements were

effective. U.S. investments alone, in mines, factories, smelters, ranches and farmlands, grew from almost nothing at the beginning of the Díaz regime to $500 million in 1902, and to something in excess of one billion dollars in 1920, more than the total capital investment owned by Mexicans. The wealthy minority lived in the midst of brocaded walls, lace curtains and gilt furniture, and boasted that there was nothing Mexican in their homes. Mexico City, they said, was another Paris—but they spent as much time as possible in the real Paris.

To celebrate the centennial of the War of Independence, in 1910 Don Porfirio invited dignitaries from all over the world to see the new and improved Mexico, the new railroads (with trains that ran on time), harbor works, drainage systems, broad boulevards, stately homes and European-style public buildings. There were parades, fireworks, balls, concerts, champagne and flowers. Indians and paupers were ordered to stay off the main streets of the capital.

Meanwhile there had been omens of death and destruction, just as there had been among the Aztecs before the Spaniards arrived. There was a violent eruption of the volcano at Colima. There were earth tremors. Night after night a fiery comet was seen in the sky. The educated people recognized it for what it was—Halley's comet—but this knowledge was limited to the minority that could read.

PEOPLE had begun to mutter, and some of the muttering was serious. In northern Mexico in 1908 a strange little man named Francisco Madero had written a book called *The Presidential Succession in 1910*, arguing mildly for political freedom for Mexico (re-election of Díaz time after time had by now become a mere formality). Madero came from one of the wealthiest families in Mexico. But he himself was more interested in humanitarian ideas than in wealth; given a cotton plantation to manage, he had spent its income on the workers, feeding their children at his own table.

His book made him the rallying point for some of the country's intellectual and political malcontents. He toured the country, arguing in his high-pitched voice against Díaz' re-election. An anti-re-electionist party was formed, and in 1910 Madero was nominated for the presidency. Díaz ordered him thrown in jail, and went on to celebrate the centennial and to declare himself elected for another term. Released from jail, Madero took refuge in the United States and pronounced Díaz' election a fraud.

IT turned out that he had started something. In the state of Chihuahua, guerrilla leaders, one of them a former cattle rustler called Pancho Villa, clashed with federal troops. In Morelos a peasant named Emiliano Zapata recruited followers and began raiding sugar plantations. There were other risings around the country, in Yucatán, Veracruz, Tabasco, Durango, Sonora, Sinaloa, Puebla, Oaxaca and Guerrero. In a sense it was a repetition of 1810, when Father Hidalgo's followers armed themselves with slings and machetes and set out to vanquish the Spanish artillery.

The intellectuals knew the issues: dictatorship, the flouting of the constitution, effective suffrage, economic repression and Mexico for the Mexicans. Around them thronged a starving peasantry, landless Indians, small ranchers, cowboys, field hands from the haciendas, shopkeepers, men who had been in trouble with the law during the Porfirian Peace. Few of them knew anything more than that they were hungry and miserable, that something was wrong with the country and this was an opportunity to act. When the U.S. writer John Reed asked one of them what he was fighting for, the man replied, "Why, it is good, fighting; you don't have to work in the mines." Some of them shouted, "Little work, much *dinero*, beans for all. *Viva* Madero!" But there were many who at first had never heard of Madero. One of the intellectuals was to write, later, that the Revolution was planned by thinkers and executed by bandits, and after a time one could not be told from the other.

Madero returned to Mexico. Federal troops sent to quell the revolutionary forces deserted

and joined them. There was a battle for Ciudad Juárez on the U.S. frontier. The revolutionists won, and representatives of Díaz promised he would resign. In Mexico City, mobs rioted in front of the National Palace, shouting for the dictator's resignation. A few days later, Díaz was on his way to exile. An interim president was appointed to hold office until elections could be held, and Francisco Madero, the valiant, high-minded little man who was to become one of the many tragic figures in Mexican history, entered Mexico City in triumph.

Madero was nominated for the presidency by the Progressive Constitutional party, and an admiring observer from the U.S. embassy reported the event as "the first untrammeled political convention ever held in this country . . . really free and open and an admirable temper was displayed." The election was equally free, and Madero overwhelmingly and honestly won his mandate from the Mexican people.

THINGS went wrong almost from the outset. Powerful forces opposed Madero: remnants of the old Díaz regime, landowners and the Catholic hierarchy; business elements, mainly foreign, for whom the American ambassador, Henry Lane Wilson, was spokesman; peasant elements, impatient for the promised redistribution of land, a promise whose urgency Madero failed to grasp; and many of his own temporary allies who had joined his movement as a matter of convenience rather than conviction. Madero's own shortcomings were grave. An idealist himself, he trusted many of the wrong people. His drive for the presidency had been directed against Díaz and the political abuses that Díaz represented; he had no clear conception of the nation's fundamental economic ills, which were even more critical. He had no head for administration, nor any capacity for political intrigue.

Within 15 months of Madero's assumption of office, Mexico City was a battleground. The heart of the city was being destroyed by an artillery barrage, troops loyal to Madero firing from the National Palace, dissident forces firing back from an armory a mile away. The dissidents gained the upper hand. Through an almost unparalleled betrayal, Madero and his vice president were arrested and forced to resign in exchange for a promise of safety for themselves, their families and their adherents.

A tough old Indian fighter and drunkard named Victoriano Huerta was responsible for Madero's betrayal. Through a series of quick shifts, Huerta managed, with the approval of U.S. Ambassador Wilson and the business elements with which Wilson was identified, to make himself president. This done, Huerta had Madero and his vice president shot down in cold blood. The wife of a U.S. diplomat wrote in her diary: "Huerta has very little natural regard for human life. This isn't a specialty of successful dictators. . . . Only by the hand of iron can this passionate, tenacious, mysterious, gifted, undisciplined race, composed of countless unlike elements, be kept in order. In the States . . . this isn't quite understood." This appeared to reflect the views of most foreigners in Mexico.

From the martyred Madero, who left office on February 19, 1913, to Alvaro Obregón, who assumed office on December 1, 1920—the first man since Díaz to enjoy a full term—Mexico had 10 presidents. Few Mexicans today can recall the names of all of them. Some of them occupied the office for no more than a few weeks, and one established a short-term record of 46 minutes. Mexico was racked again with civil war. The population dropped from 15,160,369 in 1910 to 14,334,780 in 1921, a loss of more than 800,000 persons. How much of the decrease was accounted for by violent death no one will ever know; starvation and disease took heavy tolls.

THE entire republic was in a state of perpetual upheaval. Teachers, priests, thieves, mule drivers, doctors, lawyers—everyone took up arms. Many went through the quick progression from local guerrilla leader to officer to revolutionary prominence. A ballad of the time told of the soldier who arose at 10 a.m., became

a lieutenant at 11, a captain at 12 "and at ten minutes past noon a general of a division."

It was picturesque and it was colorful and much of it seemed like a Hollywood scriptwriter's dream: dark-skinned men in huge hats and crossed cartridge belts swarmed through the land, their rifles forming a pattern with the spikes of maguey on the high horizon and the stiff stalks of corn. Men on horseback charged thunderously across the plains, rolling clouds of dust against the purple mountains. Soldiers' wives and women went with their men, breast-feeding babies, cooking meager meals on tiny charcoal fires, singing the throat-catching songs of the Revolution like *Adelita* and *Valentina*. When their men fell, they took rifles and fought in the ranks. Pajama-clad Indians, hungry for land, raided the haciendas, blew up the safes, destroyed the hateful deeds that guaranteed the land to the absentee *hacendados*—and just as quickly faded away into the shadows.

THE fighting had also a nightmare quality. Captives had the soles of their feet sliced off and were forced to run across open country until they were mercifully shot down. Some prisoners were made to attempt escape so that a revolutionary chieftain could practice his marksmanship, as coolly as another man would shoot clay pigeons. Ears were lopped off and the victims made to jig until their hearts pumped the blood from their bodies. Men were buried up to their necks in sand so that their heads would be cracked open like melons by horses' hooves when the cavalry rode over them. Others were tied to horses' tails and dragged through cobbled streets. Men known to be innocent were hanged in order to demonstrate the seriousness of demands for money. Plantation foremen were nailed to hacienda doors and left to die.

The ebb and flow in the fortunes of revolutionary leaders, their brave pronouncements and contrary actions, their mercurial alliances and sudden enmities became a maze of fact and legend, confusing to Mexicans themselves and utterly baffling to others. Almost all the leading figures of the Revolution fought each other at one time or another—Pancho Villa against Venustiano Carranza, Alvaro Obregón against Villa, Pablo González against Emiliano Zapata, Plutarco Elías Calles against José Maytorena, Obregón against Carranza, Calles against Carranza. The United States, which through the activities of Ambassador Wilson at first supported Huerta, next found itself supporting Villa and Obregón against Huerta, and later Carranza against Villa (who retaliated by raiding the U.S. territory along the border, thereby precipitating the armed intervention of U.S. forces under General Pershing).

THE most powerful figure to emerge in the early years of the Revolution was Venustiano Carranza, the white-bearded old governor of Coahuila. Carranza out-maneuvered his rival Villa for leadership of the country. As *de facto* president in 1916, he called a constitutional convention which was to produce the most important single result of the Revolution. This convention met at Querétaro and, by the end of January 1917, had drafted Mexico's fifth constitution in less than a century.

Although not all participants in the Revolution were represented in its drafting (the *Villistas* and *Zapatistas* were notably absent), the document was a truly revolutionary one, more so than the conservative-minded Carranza had wished. It reinforced the reform laws regarding public education and the activity of the Catholic Church. It declared that all land, water and other resources were the property of the republic and could be held privately only on the sufferance of the state, thus opening the way for the long-delayed redistribution of land and the expropriation of oilfields and other industry. And it adopted a highly advanced labor code governing hours, wages, working conditions, debt enslavement and the right to organize and to strike.

It was, in a sense, an *ex post facto* formulation of the basic aims of the Revolution; it gave the struggle a meaning which until then had seemed almost wholly lacking. It is still in effect today. It did not, however, bring an immediate end to Mexico's strife.

The revolutionary leaders' hold on both authority and life was precarious. Pancho Villa, the most flamboyant figure of the Revolution, began to fade away. The wild cavalry charges that had won him easy victories in the early days lost their magic. The Mexican people, no longer so afraid of him, laughed when he suggested that he and Carranza solve their differences by commiting suicide (which Villa might well have done if he had been certain Carranza would agree to it). He was persuaded to retire to his ranch. Later he was assassinated by a hired killer.

Emiliano Zapata, the least self-seeking of the revolutionary generals, stuck stubbornly to his one demand: land for his white-clad Indian followers. Implacable and unswerving, he was finally lured into a trap and shot down as treacherously as Madero had been. Many of his followers refused to believe him dead, and for many years they said that on dark nights Zapata, astride his white horse, still rode in the hills of Morelos.

Carranza in the end lost all support and fled from the presidential office, loading as much treasure as possible into a special train bound for Veracruz. The train was intercepted by one of his own men, and Carranza went into the mountains on horseback, only to be shot while sleeping on the earthen floor of an Indian hut.

MEANWHILE Alvaro Obregón, the onetime mechanic and rancher from Sonora who commanded a devoted following of tough Yaquis, proved himself the ablest general and the wiliest politician of the lot. Intelligent, good-natured and cynical, Obregón had a gift for statecraft. He had been a dominant figure in the formulation of the 1917 constitution, and he was one of the few of the revolutionary leaders equipped to lead the nation. In November 1920, he became Mexico's president, and the most disastrous but meaningful decade in the country's history was over. What Mexico bought, it had bought dearly.

REVOLUTIONARY PRIEST, Miguel Hidalgo led the first uprising against imperial Spain in 1810. He was executed but remains a symbol of Mexican independence.

A Century of Rebellion and Strife

Mexico simmered long in the backwaters of history, but after it won independence in the 19th Century an extraordinary cast of characters came onto the scene—sinister generals, devoted reformers, imperious presidents, bandit chiefs. Blunderingly, they brought the new nation into conflict with the expanding United States. Opposing Mexico in 1846, young American officers sharpened military skills later to be of use to both Blue and Gray in the Civil War; Mexico lost a large part of its northern territory and soon gained another incredible collection of dictators, exploiters and self-seeking leaders. But even more travail awaited the harassed land. In the turbulent decade of 1910-1920, the still-young nation was almost torn asunder as one half of the motley group came into bloody and violent contention with the other.

CRAFTY GENERAL, Antonio López de Santa Anna (*left*) made himself dictator in the period after independence was won in 1821. He held power on and off until 1855.

TRAGIC EMPRESS, Carlota reigned as the wife of Maximilian, the Austrian archduke who ascended the Mexican throne in 1864. She died insane in Europe in 1927.

INDIAN STATESMAN, Benito Juárez ran away from his Zapotec home as a boy. As president in the late 1860s, he laid the foundations of the public school system.

ILL-FATED EMPEROR, Maximilian I (*right*) was the unwitting tool of French forces which seized the country in 1862. He was executed by Juárez' troops in 1867.

IRON-WILLED PRESIDENT, Porfirio Díaz (*opposite, center*) strides into a 1910 reception given by U.S. Ambassador Henry Lane Wilson (*right*). Months later Díaz was out.

INEFFECTUAL REFORMER, Francisco Madero (*center*) became a rallying point for the forces which overthrew Díaz. Well-meaning but slow-acting, he was killed in 1913.

RUGGED BAND headed by one General Macias aided in the overthrow of Díaz. For a decade the Mexican countryside was alive with such groups.

BOLD CONGRESS, legislators (*left*) posed for this photo in 1913 after dictator Victoriano Huerta ordered the members jailed for calling him a tyrant.

REBEL GIRLS, these *soldaderas* accompanied Huerta's troops. Women followed the revolutionary bands and sometimes actually took part in battles.

BORDER MEETING at El Paso in 1914 brought Alvaro Obregón (*left*) and Pancho Villa together with U.S. General John Pershing (*right*), later U.S. commander in Europe in World War I. Villa's forces had been battling troops loyal to Carranza so near the U.S. border that several Americans had been wounded by stray

bullets. Villa agreed to move back from the border, but two years later, in 1916, angered by U.S. support of Carranza, he sent raiding parties into New Mexico.

WILY POLITICIAN, bearded Venustiano Carranza, who became president in 1917, confers with a successor, Obregón, who had lost an arm during a 1915 battle.

5

A One-Party Democracy

THE Mexican Revolution, a profound and continuing transformation, is well into its second half century. Mexico was one of the first of many underdeveloped countries in the world which in the 20th Century rebelled against the iniquities of the past in a struggle for the modern statehood that the past had denied them. The first half century of the struggle in Mexico was divided into four somewhat unequal parts: a stretch of disastrous internal war (see Chapter 4), the recovery of the wrecked nation, the translating of the Revolution's philosophy into specific objectives and a period of progress toward those objectives.

"We have had enough of killing in Mexico," the late Luis Cabrera, one of the tough-minded idealists of the Revolution, said after the fighting ceased. "We do not propose to kill; we propose to live, and to make certain that the diverse component parts of our nation shall go on living, growing and multiplying for the aggrandizement of our fatherland."

At Chapultepec in Mexico City, one of the world's truly great parks, the Mexican ministry of education maintains for the public a handsome and well-planned gallery of history. Visitors follow a descending ramp past a series of dioramas that trace, in detail, the troubled history of Mexico from the beginnings of the War of Independence in 1810 to the adoption of the constitution of 1917—the charter of the Revolution and of modern Mexico. At the press of a button each diorama is illuminated, in turn, and a recorded voice explains in simple language the great events: the martyrdom of Hidalgo and Morelos, the War of Reform, the French imposition of Maximilian, the hopes of Juárez, the Díaz dictatorship and the explosive Revolution.

At the end of the long ramp the visitors—on Sundays and holidays the crowds are tremendous—emerge into a round, high-ceilinged room. Mexicans young and old invariably gasp when they enter, so stirring is the effect. The walls are of dull red *tezontle*, a kind of lava rock. Light filters down through a red glass ceiling. Against one wall is a stark white stone carving of the Mexican eagle, its wings outspread, the serpent in its mouth. Under the eagle in a heavy silver case is the Mexican constitution, the achievement of a century of torment. Even the visitor from outside Mexico is struck with awe and wonder and with sympathy for a people whose struggle has been so great.

THE exhibition does not, however, provide either a chronology or an evaluation of events later than 1917, the period during which modern Mexico has actually taken shape and substance. One difficulty is that many of the men who directed Mexico's course in the early years of this period are still alive, thereby making historical perspective difficult. Yesterday's heroes and triumphs can become—as they frequently have become in the country's past—tomorrow's scoundrels and disasters, and vice versa. More significantly, the evolution of government and democracy in Mexico has been unique, and judgment by comparative standards is necessarily inconclusive. A detached point of view is always difficult to achieve and almost impossible to maintain.

A Mexican psychoanalyst, Francisco González Piñeda, recently took an analytical look at his nation and, in a little book entitled

The Mexican, His Psychosocial Dynamics, attempted to sum it up. "What kind of governmental system do we have?" he asked. "Some call it presidentialism. A prime characteristic is that its formation and rude organization are totally different from that envisioned by the constitution, which nevertheless is preserved zealously. The regime has many characteristics of absolute monarchy since all the power resides in the president and is hereditary. The inheritance does not follow blood lines or primogeniture, but follows the line of closest political and friendship ties to the incumbent president and to the ex-presidents who still retain influence. In its relation to different cultural, racial and social groups the regime has imperial characteristics. . . . It is sectarian because it carries out policy through a party with a doctrinaire base that excludes any other political possibility for the nation. It is demagogic because it justifies itself with doctrinary postulates which it ignores or denies in reality. However, the regime is also realistic because in its own way it tries to solve some of the country's problems. . . ."

The Mexican government wears many of the trappings of totalitarianism, yet it is not totalitarian; if it were truly so it would never have permitted González Piñeda to publish his book openly, which he did. Nor would it allow Mexicans to speak out, as they have done and still do almost constantly, criticizing Mexico's version of democracy.

THE faults, nevertheless, are easily found. Only one party, the *Partido Revolucionario Institucional,* or PRI, has any meaningful existence. The office of the presidency is vested with autocratic power, usually exercised benignly but nevertheless still virtually absolute. Over the years, most presidents have picked their own successors, and the official party has gone ahead to implement the choice through rigidly controlled election machinery. The private citizen's vote—the "effective suffrage" which has become a byword of Mexican political philosophy—more often than not merely affirms decisions that have already been made.

Checks and balances on the executive, in the sense in which they are known elsewhere, are almost nonexistent. Congressional authority and legislative processes are ostentatious and noisy but not particularly effective. The courts, while respected, enjoy little independence. Free self-government at the state and municipal level is freakishly rare. Freedom of speech and press is observed, but the impact is minimal. The "revolutionary" politician who does not enrich himself in office is sufficiently unusual to be regarded with either extraordinary admiration or a combination of pity and contempt. The *mordida,* or bite (the bribery of an official), exists throughout the government.

YET these characteristics, melancholy as they may appear to the lover of simon-pure, classic democracy, are deceptive. With them, or despite them, Mexico has achieved a degree of democracy that among Latin American republics is remarkable for its effectiveness and stability. The government's concern for the basic problems of the nation is genuine, and its progress toward the solution of those problems, although erratic at times, is real. If this were not the case, Mexico would not enjoy, as it does, the public service of brilliant, selfless men —lawyers, teachers, poets, engineers, economists, novelists, industrialists—who give everything that they have in the way of intellectual and physical resources to help achieve the humanitarian ends of the Mexican Revolution. Such people endure bureaucratic inefficiency, flagrant corruption and civic feather-bedding in the hope that such ills will in due course be cured. To eradicate all of these evils at once would, in all likelihood, plunge Mexico into another bloody conflict.

The first years of postrevolutionary peace in Mexico were dominated by two men—Alvaro Obregón, the most successful general of the Revolution, and Plutarco Elías Calles, a one-time schoolteacher and bartender. Both were hardened by war and experienced in revolutionary ways. Both had been supporters of

Venustiano Carranza, and both were later leaders of the forces that drove Carranza from his office and to his death. For a time it appeared that the two leaders, alternating the presidency between them, might dominate Mexico for decades to come.

THE Obregón-Calles period was a peaceful one—but only in comparison with the extraordinarily violent years that had gone before. The habit of conspiracy had become well established. *Pronunciamentos* and *cuartelazos,* uprisings and garrison revolts, were a way of life. Both Obregón and Calles put them down with a hard hand, and the work of reconstruction went on. Obregón, a self-taught genius as a military commander, proved to be a remarkable politician, full of common sense, ambitious for his country as well as for himself, practical and good-humored. Asked what had become of all the bandits who were supposed to be roaming the Mexican countryside, Obregón replied that when he had come to the capital as president all the bandits had come with him. Potentially troublesome old revolutionary leaders were placed in soft jobs where they could enrich themselves in tranquillity while Obregón went about his business.

The President had been one of the principal backers of the 1917 constitution, and he now set about putting it into effect throughout the country. An ambitious program of free public education was launched. Labor was encouraged to organize, as were the peasants, to whom the government was distributing expropriated land. Both groups became bulwarks of the government—and they have remained so. When one of the groups threatened to get out of hand, Obregón and his successor would use the other as a counterweight.

Calles had served Obregón as minister of *gobernación,* or interior, the top-ranking cabinet post in the government, and was hand-picked by Obregón as his successor. The choice triggered a three-month rebellion, put down with the help of arms and ammunition which Obregón had managed to obtain from the U.S., along with formal diplomatic recognition.

Calles lacked Obregón's charm but, at first, none of his predecessor's revolutionary zeal. He continued the programs which Obregón had started, built highways, launched irrigation projects, founded a national bank, balanced the budget and made substantial progress in paying off debts, both internal and foreign. Promulgation of laws to activate the constitution projected him into two major conflicts, one with the foreign oil companies (which was smoothed out later by U.S. Ambassador Dwight Morrow), the other with the Catholic Church. The latter was to be a climactic event in Mexican history, the decisive battle in a war that had been going on for more than a century.

IN colonial Mexico the Catholic Church had occupied a position that was in many ways equal to that of the viceroyal government. Its status was official, supreme and unchallenged. The position of the Church was weakened in the 19th Century by the reform laws and by the Juárez administration, but its hold on the Mexican people continued to be deep and strong. Mexican Catholicism might differ in marked degree from more conventional varieties of the faith, but the country was overwhelmingly Catholic. The Church clearly felt itself to be independent of the government, and early in 1926 the archbishop of Mexico publicly repudiated Mexico's new constitution. In retaliation the government deported 200 foreign-born priests and nuns, ordered all others to register with civil authorities and closed parochial primary schools. Catholics throughout Mexico were enraged. The Church struck back by in effect going on strike, and for three years no church services were held in Mexico.

The government was in the awkward position of constitutionally guaranteeing freedom of worship but seemingly denying people the solace of the only church that had any meaning for them. In the western states of Michoacán, Jalisco and Colima, the *Cristero* movement assumed alarming proportions. The *Cristeros*, shouting "Long live Christ the King!" burned

schools, stole government funds and once even dynamited a railroad train, killing 100 persons. The government exiled half a dozen Catholic bishops and sent troops to execute a brutal scorched-earth policy in the *Cristero* country.

In 1928, at the end of the four-year Calles administration (the presidential term was thereafter increased to six years), Obregón appeared to be the only man sufficiently strong to rescue Mexico from the disorder into which the religious conflict had plunged it. He had also been somewhat more conciliatory toward the Church than had Calles. The constitution was amended to get around the ban on re-election, and to no one's surprise Obregón was elected. Before he could take office, however, he was shot down by a young Catholic fanatic.

The tide of anticlericalism that had been rising in Mexico since the early 19th Century reached a high point in the trial of the assassin and the alleged conspirators. Then, slowly, it began to recede. In the Lázaro Cárdenas administration of 1934-1940, there were gestures of *rapprochement* between government and Church. President Manuel Avila Camacho (1940-1946) avowed his own Catholicism early in his administration, and soon it became respectable for officials to admit their religious affiliations. In succeeding administrations there has been, if not reconciliation, at least a demonstration that the government of the Mexican people and the Church to which 95 per cent of them belong can live together in peace.

ANTICLERICAL laws are still on the books today, empowering the states to limit the number of priests, banning the public wearing of clerical garb and setting down strictures on Catholic education and Church activities. But the government tends to look the other way. In one instance an order of Catholic nursing sisters who had been forced to leave Mexico in 1875 and had taken refuge in France was officially invited to return and take charge of a poorly run hospital, and return they did. Under several progressive archbishops the Church, for its part, has adopted a more moderate attitude toward the state, urging Mexican Catholics to be true to their government and even officially honoring as national heroes the excommunicated priests Hidalgo and Morelos (without, however, actually naming them).

The Catholic-oriented political party, *Partido Acción Nacional* or PAN, is not only tolerated by the government but is even allowed to elect a few members to the national legislature in each election. The PAN delegation in no way threatens the power of the official PRI, but it does voice complaints and criticisms which the government party of a few decades ago would not have permitted.

The one-party system began in the decade immediately following the Revolution. Numerous political parties had been in existence since the time of Mexico's independence, but most of them were short-lived. Usually they came into being to wage an election campaign, to support the ambitions or ideas of one man or to press a single issue. With the campaign won or lost, the candidate in office, in exile or dead, or the issue resolved, they usually disappeared. Only the army enjoyed any continuity as a political organization. Calles and Obregón both recognized the need for a permanent party which would incorporate all the elements necessary for carrying out the program of the Revolution—peasants, workers and politicians as well as revolutionary generals.

Calles had another reason, moreover, for wanting to form a new organization. With Obregón dead, Calles had no intention of relinquishing his position as a power behind the presidency. A continuing political party was a necessity. The *Partido Nacional Revolucionario* came into being in 1929. Although the

name has been changed twice since then—to the *Partido de la Revolución Mexicana* in 1938 and to the *Partido Revolucionario Institucional* (PRI) in 1946—essentially the same party governs Mexico today. Changes have taken place in its character and composition, most of them for the better. Although elections are still tightly controlled, opposition candidates and their supporters are seldom given the rough treatment that was once commonplace. The PRI has indicated that, in addition to tolerating a congressional opposition, it will permit free elections of state and local governments.

The PRI is also developing a sensitivity to public feeling and has made adjustments in its policies and programs accordingly. When the population of Oaxaca in 1952 rebelled against a governor whom the PRI had imposed, the PRI retreated and the governor was removed.

The presidents of Mexico may still be selected by their predecessors and his party chiefs, but variations among their individual personalities reveal shifts in the disposition of the PRI. The last five chief executives, while dedicated to the aims of the Revolution, have all been moderate, conciliatory men. The last four have been civilians, indicating that the army, once dominant in Mexican affairs, has retreated to the position of supporting policy instead of dictating it. President Adolfo López Mateos, far from being a general or an old revolutionary, was born the year the Revolution began. His chosen successor, Gustavo Díaz Ordaz, who was elected in 1964, is a lawyer with a reputation as an efficient administrator in a long succession of government jobs. The official party today has within its ranks representatives of all groups—laborers and industrialists, *ejidatarios*

PRESIDENTS OF MEXICO SINCE 1920

Alvaro Obregón	1920-1924
Plutarco Elías Calles	1924-1928
Emilio Portes Gil	1928-1930
Pascual Ortiz Rubio	1930-1932
Abelardo L. Rodríguez	1932-1934
Lázaro Cárdenas	1934-1940
Manuel Avila Camacho	1940-1946
Miguel Alemán	1946-1952
Adolfo Ruiz Cortines	1952-1958
Adolfo López Mateos	1958-1964
Gustavo Díaz Ordaz	1964-

CHIEF EXECUTIVES of recent years are listed above. Three men served short terms from 1928 to 1934 after President-elect Obregón was shot.

and landowners, intellectuals and military men, Communists and conservatives, atheists and Catholics. Some theorists believe Mexico may in time develop three effective organizations—left, center and right. If that comes to pass, the PRI might lose members who now participate solely because it is the only party which plays an important political role. But the PRI would without question remain a powerful centrist organization.

Although it has remained revolutionary in name and principle, the PRI has swung like a pendulum between left and right in its specific programs. It reached its extreme leftward position in the selection of General Lázaro Cárdenas as president of Mexico in 1934.

Cárdenas was to become the most significant president in post-Revolution Mexico. Although it was he who enunciated the principle that ex-presidents should stay out of politics and allow the incumbent a free hand, his influence extended far beyond his term of office, and modern Mexico cannot be understood without recognition of the role Cárdenas plays. His name still has much luster with the people, and he has frequently been called "the conscience of the Revolution." Whenever the official party appears to be swinging too far to the right, Cárdenas' influence comes into play as a corrective. He has continued to be the expression of something profoundly Mexican.

TO understand how Cárdenas came to power, it is necessary to return for a moment to Plutarco Elías Calles, the ex-president. After Obregón's death in 1928, Calles had remained the *jefe maximo,* or boss, of the country—even though others occupied the presidential office. Formerly a radical, Calles grew more and more conservative—possibly, it is said, through the influence of his good friend, U.S. Ambassador Morrow. He became convinced that the redistribution of land—an integral part of the revolutionary program and one he had earlier pursued—was inefficient, and the program came almost to a halt. He and his friends grew rich, acquiring landholdings and erecting mansions for them-

selves (the neighborhood in which most of them built their homes became known as the Street of the Forty Thieves). Socialist Mexico swung toward the sort of capitalism that had not flourished since the days of Porfirio Díaz.

There was public grumbling, and leaders of the official party felt that a change in course was indicated, a return to the first principles of the Revolution. They found their man in Cárdenas. From the standpoint of his career he had everything a successful politician needed. A guerrilla fighter in the Revolution when he was little more than a boy, he had risen to the rank of general by the time he was 25. He had been active in the party; was popular with the army, the peasants and the workers; and had been a state governor, minister of the interior and minister of war.

AT this point, however, Cárdenas departed from the norm. He was closemouthed, inscrutable, puritanical and scrupulously honest. He had accumulated none of the wealth that was rapidly becoming the badge of the old revolutionaries. His elevation to the presidency by the party that Calles had created was one of the paradoxes that stud Mexican history like cactus spines. Early in his administration he cut off the sources of enrichment and power of Calles and his cronies, and he followed this up by unceremoniously throwing Calles and the corrupt labor boss Luis Morones out of the country.

As a presidential candidate he had traveled throughout Mexico, by train, car or horse or on foot, talking with local groups and individuals about their problems (a practice copied by later candidates). After his election he continued his moving about, and it was said that he was more genuinely concerned with a peasant's sick cow or a village's lack of a school than he was with crises in the national bank or in foreign affairs. He reactivated the expropriation and distribution of land and pursued the policy relentlessly. He ordered the national telegraph system to accept free of charge for one hour a day all wires from poor folk addressed to the president.

People with bare feet or sandals were always the first to be ushered from the waiting room into the presidential office, while generals and politicians flicked the dust from their boots. Cárdenas refused to live in the presidential palace at Chapultepec. He talked to common soldiers without arranging it through their generals, to laborers without consulting the union bosses, to peasants without going through the agrarian leaders. He developed tremendous loyalties among the working people of Mexico—loyalties which still remain strong. Among the Indians of his native Michoacán he is known as Tata Lázaro, or Daddy Lázaro, just as the great 16th Century bishop, Vasco de Quiroga, had been known as Tata Vasco.

As an outgrowth of an oil workers' strike, Cárdenas expropriated foreign-owned oil properties. Almost overnight he became a controversial figure on the world scene and a symbol of Leftism in Mexico—an identification he did nothing to discourage. He has frequently been a spokesman for the extreme Left in Mexico, and has often been labeled a Communist. This is an oversimplification of a complex character. Cárdenas has been more than friendly with Russia, subscribes to many Marxist theories and once received the Stalin Peace Prize. But he was also the man who welcomed anti-Stalinist Leon Trotsky to political asylum in Mexico.

He aided the migration to Mexico of countless Spanish Republican refugees, most of them bitterly anticlerical after the Spanish Civil War; but he was also responsible for the reopening of many church doors in Mexico and has been a close friend of many dignitaries of the Catholic Church. Today Cárdenas remains, among Mexicans and foreigners alike, one of the most controversial figures in modern Mexican history.

CARDENAS is also regarded, with justification, as an exponent of anti-United States feeling in Mexico. The gravity with which these sentiments should be viewed is debatable. Anti-gringoism ("gringo" is Mexican slang for a person from the U.S.) is not a new thing and is not a product of the Cold War. It is,

instead, almost as old as Mexico's independence. Nor is it constant: it waxes and wanes with the times. The United States, having been responsible for a fair share of Mexico's historical griefs, is a handy scapegoat for all of them, just as the most wealthy and powerful man in any community is, more often than not, blamed for all of the community's ills, regardless of the origin of those ills. An incident of discrimination against Mexicans in the United States, a crisis in U.S. relations with another Latin American republic, or for that matter an emotional storm having no apparent connection with the United States—any one of these can produce student demonstrations in front of the United States embassy in Mexico, angry speeches and shouts of "Mexico for Mexicans!" Such responses are, of course, encouraged and skillfully utilized by the Communists.

BUT a number of things must be put in the balance against the ill feeling: U.S. loans and technical assistance; the work of U.S. foundations in such areas as agriculture, education and hygiene; investment of private U.S. capital in Mexican industry; exchanges of college students; settlement of the long-standing Chamizal border dispute; and the many meetings of U.S. and Mexican presidents. Even the much-maligned U.S. tourist can become a factor for greater understanding when he behaves with dignity, restraint and friendly interest.

Ill feeling diminishes with understanding, and the governments of the U.S. and Mexico are working hard for greater accord in areas of mutual concern. The evolutionary process that created Mexico's strange one-party democracy is also producing political maturity. It is a maturity that may have substantial meaning for the entire Western Hemisphere. Many influential Mexicans have expressed the hope that Mexico, which is so intimately associated with the United States in geography, history and economics, may in time become an instrument for greater harmony and sympathy between the United States and the other Latin American republics.

GIANT ELECTION RALLY staged in the city of Puebla's 45,000-seat soccer stadium draws workers and farmers to hear presidential candidate Gustavo Díaz Ordaz speak before the 1964 election. Although he had no real opposition, he campaigned in all corners of the country.

An Odd Passion for Politics

In politics, as in many other areas, Mexico is at once intense and contradictory. The one-party democracy allows only the nominees of the Partido Revolucionario Institucional to hope for election to major offices, yet PRI candidates stump the poster-plastered land as if about to be overwhelmed by the opposition. Rallies draw thousands, and the inauguration is filled with pomp and splendor. Despite such political fireworks, recent presidents have not been demagogues but hard-working men devoted to improving the people's lot with far-reaching social security programs and land reforms.

VOTER REGISTRATION attracts a line of Mexico City workers. To register, a man need not give proof of age, literacy or citizenship. Despite the country's one-party system, the people follow the campaigning with interest, and an amazing 70 per cent of the electorate votes.

BLIZZARD OF CONFETTI is part of a tumultuous reception organized in behalf of presidential candidate Gustavo Díaz Ordaz, riding through Puebla streets with his wife during the 1964 campaign. The president-to-be began his career as a city official and magistrate in Puebla.

but there remains a basic friendliness

WITH A WARM HUG, U.S. President Johnson and Mexican President López Mateos greet each other in 1964 in celebration of a treaty returning 437 acres of borderland claimed by Mexico. Partially hidden in the background, Lady Bird Johnson embraces Señora López Mateos.

WITH ANGRY SLOGANS, a crowd of Mexican students demonstrates against U.S. policies toward Cuba in 1961. The students carry caricatures of the then President Kennedy and of Premier Castro, and banners proclaiming that the U.S. must not intervene in the affairs of Cuba.

MEDICAL CONSULTATION is given a mother and her daughter by a doctor in the clinic at Unidad Morelos. The clinic is open 24 hours a day to handle emergencies.

CALISTHENICS CLASS for girls does exercises next to the center's enormous swimming pool *(above)*. Unidad Morelos has athletic programs for people of all ages.

FOLK DANCING LESSONS amuse a class of girls *(below)* t the center. Families that qualify for Mexico's Social ecurity system may use the facilities of such centers.

VAST WELFARE PROGRAM includes centers like Mexico City's Unidad Morelos which provide clinics, classes and sports

CARPENTRY WORKSHOP draws men who wish to better themselves by learning a new trade. The center also has classes in welding and other needed industrial skills.

DEBATING SOCIETY meets in the library at Unidad Morelos. The society is growing fast, and has had great success in stimulating young men to read and study.

SHOPPERS, members of a middle-class family (*left*) inspect wares in the commissary of a brewery in Monterrey where the father works as a salesman.

LABORERS trained in a state-owned factory in Hidalgo (*opposite*) lunch in the cafeteria. The mural recalls rights guaranteed by the constitution.

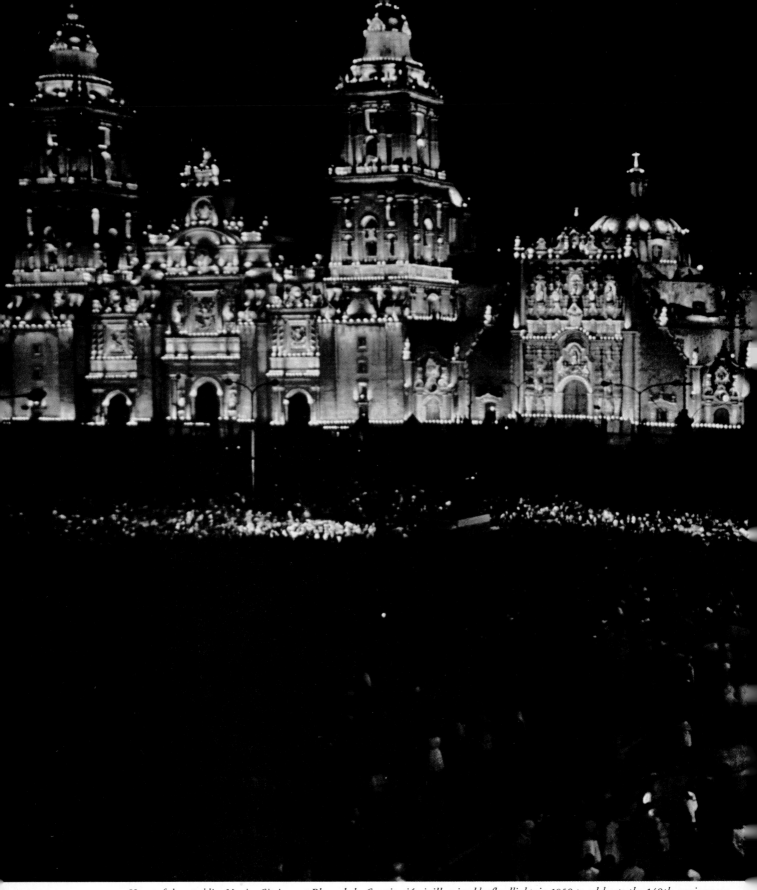

Heart of the republic, Mexico City's great Plaza de la Constitución is illumined by floodlights in 1958 to celebrate the 148th anniversary

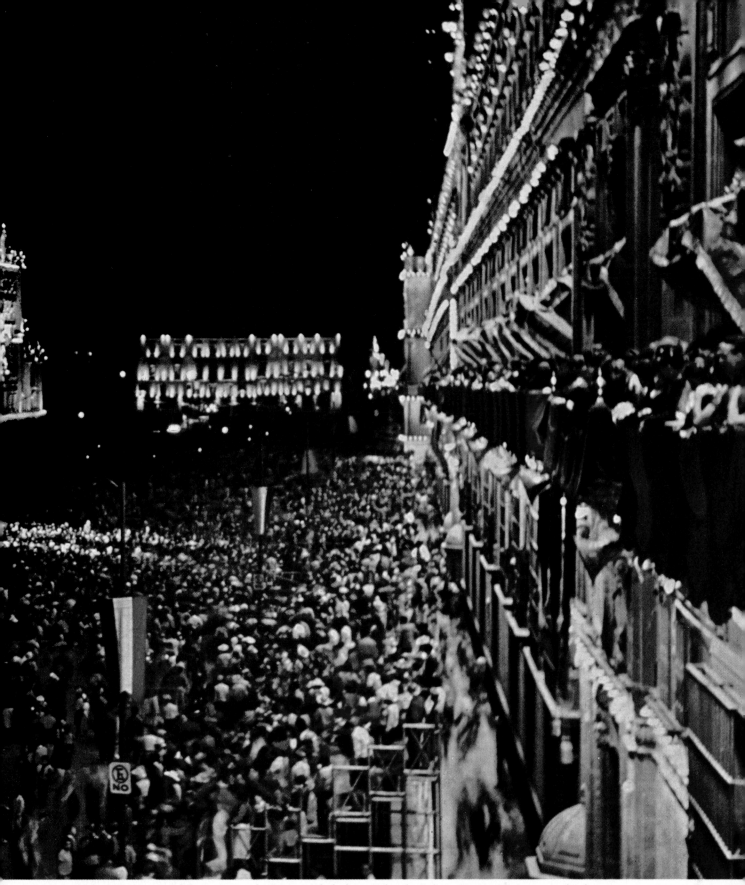
of the revolt against Spain. At left is the city's 17th Century cathedral, at right, the Palacio Nacional, government headquarters.

6

The Bond with the Earth

FOR the Mexican, the earth has always had a mystical quality. Among the Aztecs, the gesture of touching a forefinger to the earth and then to the tongue was a sign of deference and homage and, at the same time, an oath of honesty, the most solemn that could be made. The word *tierra,* or land, was always the most evocative battle cry in Mexico's revolutions and civil wars: land and liberty, land and water, land and schools, land and books, land and roads. Land was the common denominator of revolutionary dreams.

The child of rural Mexico is carried to the fields in infancy, wrapped up in his mother's *rebozo.* The breast that feeds him has the fragrance of the earth. His first memories are of his parents, his elder brothers and his sisters working the soil. His first toys are pebbles and blades of grass. Soon after he can stand erect he learns to handle the *coa,* the primitive all-purpose farming tool. Before he learns his ABCs —if he ever has the opportunity to do so—he finds out how to read the clouds and their promise of rain, and to tell, by running dry soil through his fingers, how soon the warmth of the earth will produce a crop. He discovers that the wooden *santo,* or holy figure, must be taken from the church and carried through the village at the proper time to ensure rainfall; he may also learn rituals and prayers in the old tongue to propitiate Tlaloc, god of rain. His whole life is tied to the soil, as was his father's and his father's father's, back into the dim past.

The bond with the soil is a strong one. In part it springs from the scarcity of tillable earth in a country that is for the most part mountain and desert. Productive earth is precious to a degree little understood in countries more amply endowed; it is a thing a man will, if necessary, give his life to secure, protect and keep. The Mexican's bond with the earth also springs from his enslavement to one of the most tyrannical of all crops: maize, or corn.

MAIZE," says the agricultural economist Edmundo Flores, "is the most important single item in Mexico's diet, cuisine, mythology and politics. It is a basic need . . . a dietary obsession and a nightmare for the minister of agriculture."

At least 4,000 years ago, the aboriginal people of Mexico had learned that certain cereal grasses produced heads of edible seeds that could be harvested and ground to produce meal or stored safely for planting in the next season. The discovery of a staple crop was a turning point in the evolution of these people, just as it was in the ancient cultures of Europe and Asia. Nomads became settlers and built houses, villages and cities. Liberation from the ceaseless search for food provided leisure; between crops the ancient Americans could turn their minds to developing new techniques, to arts and crafts, to contemplative thought and to study. The sun, wind, rain, fire, light and darkness all played a part in producing crops, and they became personified as gods to be honored, pleased and obeyed. Men who could explain the gods became priests; if the priests said the gods demanded human sacrifice, the maize farmers turned warrior and raided neighboring peoples for captives to be immolated in the temples.

When migrations or conquests made more land available for clearing and planting maize, cities grew and flourished. But when drought, diseases, insect pests or exhaustion of the soil stopped the work of the maize farmer for an extended period, the people would drift away, seeking other lands and other climates, and the cities would fall into ruin. Ceremonial halls, temples, astronomical observatories and pyramids would be abandoned to creeping jungle growth or drifting dust.

THE cycle of clearing the land, planting maize, exhausting the soil and moving on was one that was repeated through thousands of years, down into modern recorded history. It was a process that had a cumulative effect. At first the cycle was not very destructive. The soil in the oldest maize culture was still rich in humus. The ancient Mexican burned off the trees and brush and planted his grains of maize by punching holes in the earth with a stick. The earth retained most of its humus and the soil's depletion was delayed. But when the first land was no longer fruitful or when other pressures came into play, the farmer moved on to new land, land that often was less desirable and that was more easily and quickly exhausted.

It was a progression that was to be inexorably speeded by the arrival of the white man. For one thing, the white man brought beasts of burden and the plow, both vastly more efficient than anything the farmer had ever seen, but both lending themselves to more rapid destruction of the soil. To build New Spain, the Hispanic conquerors cut timber from the steep mountainsides—timber that the aborigines had always considered inviolate, since it helped to store water underground against the dry seasons. Maize fields moved up into the hills, beginning the process of erosion that would in time lay bare the sterile skeleton of the earth.

But a greater pressure on land-poor Mexico was exerted by the establishment of plantation-like haciendas by the Spaniards. Great estates could be created only by dispossessing the Indians. Cortés himself at one point owned estates whose area totaled 25,000 square miles. *Encomiendas*—entrustments of Indians for working the land—engulfed entire villages.

Under the system that had been operative in many of the old Indian cultures, land was owned communally by a village. Families were allotted parcels of land to farm for their own support, while ownership rested with the village. Gradually overlords, nobles, warriors and priests began to acquire shares of the common property with the rights of ownership instead of mere use. As a result, commoners frequently were deprived of land and many became serfs—the beginning of a landless peasantry. Although it is popular to blame the Spanish for all the ills that befell the Indians, the accusation should at least be qualified. The Spaniards simply intensified a system of serfdom that had begun to develop among the Indians themselves.

THROUGH the three centuries of colonialism, the amount of land suitable and available for cultivation diminished steadily, while the institution of serfdom kept increasing. Periodically there were royal decrees restoring ancestral lands to the Indians, but the decrees were easily ignored or, after a time, forgotten. One village, founded in 1369 but dispersed by the Conquest, had reassembled itself on its old lands by the early years of the 17th Century. Later, without the inhabitants' knowledge, a bribed judge permitted the village lands to be sold to a Spaniard. It was not until 1860 that the 4,000 landless Indians were able to re-establish their title.

The *hacendados* were not the only large landowners. The Roman Catholic Church, which through its missionaries had done so much to better the sorry state of the Indians in the early days of colonialism, had itself become the greatest of all landowners by the beginning of the 19th Century. At the time the War of Independence started, in 1810, the Catholic Church owned at least half of the real property and capital of Mexico and, through mortgages and other loans, controlled a considerable portion of the remainder. The Church had received outright grants of land from the Crown as well as grants of native labor to build its churches, residences, schools, hospitals, monasteries and convents. Half of the

cost of such building was borne by the Crown and half by the Spanish settlers, while the Indian construction labor was free. Tithes, bequests, gifts, fees and alms helped swell the Church's wealth. In the diocese of Puebla, always an area of great Catholic power, four fifths of the real property was said to belong to the Church. One Catholic order owned haciendas stretching in an unbroken line from Mexico City to Tampico, a distance of more than 400 miles.

The reform laws of 1856 and the constitution of 1857 tried to break up this concentrated power. Churches and corporations were ordered to divest themselves of property. The order also covered the landowning Indian villages, apparently with the benign intention of stimulating small private holdings instead of the old communal ownership. It was thought that such a program might promote the development of a middle class. The result was that both Church lands and Indian lands were bought up by hacienda owners. Indians who had managed for many generations to subsist on village lands were forced to join the growing ranks of landless peasants. Deprived of the land that was their only way of life, they were baffled by the laws, resentful and desolate.

THE concentration of land ownership was intensified during the long Díaz dictatorship. By the end of the Díaz regime, it was estimated that more than 90 per cent of the rural families in Mexico were landless. Most of Mexico's usable land was controlled by some 8,000 haciendas. Ten of them contained approximately a quarter of a million acres apiece; one contained more than 600,000 acres; more than 150 others had 60,000 to 75,000 acres apiece; and 300 others had at least 25,000 acres.

For the hacienda owners, life was a thing of graciousness and luxury. Much of the time, however, the owners were not even present. The peasants, who worked the hacienda under the stern rule of major-domos, led lives of utter poverty. Their necessities came from the hacienda stores, and their accumulated debts were passed down from one generation to another. Some who showed a disposition to attempt escape were chained up for the night at the end of the long day's labor.

The few Indians who managed to hold on to their ancestral lands did so precariously. The scarcity of land magnified disagreements. The shifting of a *mojonera,* or boundary stone, could lead to murder. Family and village feuds that began over land disputes survive today, the original cause forgotten. The Indians had become an unstable, angry mass, quick to follow any leader who promised them land.

THE Madero movement in 1910, which ushered in the Revolution, did little to give them hope, and the ablest of the Indian leaders, Emiliano Zapata, led a revolt against the Madero government. Grim Indians from most of central Mexico joined him, their rifles well oiled, their machetes razor-sharp. Zapata proclaimed his Plan of Ayala, written for him by a village schoolmaster: "Let Señor Madero—and with him all the world—know that we shall not lay down our arms until the *ejidos* of our villages are restored to us, until we are given back the lands which the *hacendados* stole from us during the dictatorship of Porfirio Díaz, when justice was subjected to his caprice. We shall not lay down our arms until we cease to be unhappy tributaries of the despotic magnates and landholders. . . ."

Zapata and his men proposed immediate repossession of the land, and suited their actions to the proposition. The smoke of burning haciendas darkened the skies. But, unlike some of their loot-mad brethren in other revolutionary forces, the *Zapatistas* wanted nothing more than the land itself. Having seized a hacienda, they would divide up the land and forsake soldiering for plowing and planting. They were the most single-minded of the revolutionaries. Unlike the *Villistas* with their bloodcurdling cavalry charges, unlike the *Carrancistas* with their machine guns, the *Zapatistas* were guerrilla fighters who could rise from the earth to fight and just as quickly disappear into it. While the

Villistas sang of *Adelita,* whom they would take to a dance in a new silk dress, the *Zapatistas* huddled around their fires in mountain hideaways and sang, "If I am to die tomorrow let them kill me right away."

It was the stubborn, land-hungry *Zapatistas* who forced Carranza, a conservative landowner himself, to issue in 1915 the first formal decree of the Revolution aimed at agrarian reform and redistribution of land. The original decree did little actually to restore land to the masses, but it paved the way for Article 27 of the Mexican constitution, upon which all subsequent efforts to achieve land reform have been based.

The basis of Article 27 and of redistribution was the *ejido,* an outgrowth of the pre-Hispanic concept of the *altepetlalli,* village-owned communal land. Under early Spanish rule the typical unit consisted not only of the village, but also of approximately a square league (4,390 acres) of cropland, pasture and woodland—enough, presumably, to support the villagers. Portions of land were granted villagers for their lifetime and could be inherited by their sons, but failure to use the land brought forfeiture. Such land could not be sold or mortgaged.

LAND redistribution began falteringly under Carranza, picked up speed in the administrations of Alvaro Obregón and Plutarco Elías Calles, and hit a peak in the administration of Lázaro Cárdenas (1934-1940). In his six years in office, Cárdenas distributed more than 44 million acres of land and settled on it 814,519 previously landless farmers. To date, the Mexican government has expropriated a total of about 130 million acres of land and distributed it to more than 2.7 million families, or about 11 million persons, only a little less than a fourth of the population. It has also given legal title to an additional 120 million acres of land to squatters who have occupied it.

Land reform and the *ejido* system have not been without problems. Like almost everything else in the Revolution, the plan was conceived hurriedly to meet a critical need, and its execution has, more often than not, followed the trial and error method. The units of land made available were often too small to be farmed economically. In many cases the *ejidatarios*, or *ejido* farmers, were ill-equipped to do any farming. Some, through ignorance, were victimized by self-styled peasant leaders and ended up little better off than they had been under the hacienda system. Government organizations responsible for supplying them with credit and equipment have on occasion been paralyzed by corruption.

GRADUALLY the *ejido* problems are being worked out. The size of the parcels of land given to *ejidatarios* has been steadily increased. Credit societies and cooperatives have been formed (some *ejidos* are operated on a collective basis, but they are a minority). The original concept of grants consisting mainly of cropland has been expanded to permit integrated farming; *ejidos* based on cattle raising and forestry have been created.

The last of the truly large private landholdings to be expropriated and distributed (no others of comparable size remain) was the 647,000-acre Greene Cananea ranch, lying along the Arizona border in the state of Sonora. When the vast ranch was converted into Mexico's first collectivized cattle *ejido* in 1959, President Adolfo López Mateos told the newly created cowboy-*ejidatarios*: "You have in your hands a wealth for living; you have also an opportunity to honor the Mexican Revolution."

Not all private land has been expropriated, nor has all the expropriated land gone into *ejidos*. Private individuals may still own as much as 250 acres of humid or irrigated land or 500 acres of arid land, with no fear of expropriation. And within certain limits, individuals can purchase land as "colonists" from the government. On the whole, the production record of the colonists and the private landowners has been somewhat better than that of the *ejidos*.

In recent years Mexican agricultural production has gone up steadily. At the same time it has become much more diversified. Although maize remains—and will remain—the principal product by a vast margin, its old tyranny has lessened. Other crops have gained, and the rising export value of cotton, coffee, wheat, sugar and tomatoes in particular has done much to improve Mexico's economy.

There is widespread feeling that the *ejido* system is too limited, that it will not permit the sort of expansion and versatility needed to feed and support a rapidly growing modern nation. If this proves true, the system may become a delicate problem for the Mexican government, since the *ejido* is regarded as a key element in the Revolution. But no one in Mexico today doubts the fact that land reform, fumbling and inefficient though it has been at times, was necessary if Mexico was to take its place as a modern democracy. The Revolution abolished the old system, under which nine Mexicans out of 10 were held in virtual slavery. The old landholding class, conservative to its core and unfalteringly opposed to the Revolution, was, if not destroyed, neutralized as a political force. And much of the unstable mass of Mexican peasantry, a potentially dangerous element, was converted into a large and dependable factor of the Revolution in whose name the country is governed.

BUT agrarian reform did not solve an even more chronic problem: the acute shortage of usable land. Mexico's population is growing at the explosive rate of more than 3 per cent a year. For nationalistic reasons Mexico is proud of this growth, which represents great progress in lowering the infant mortality rate, increasing life expectancy and controlling diseases. But the pride is shadowed with worry, and rightfully so. It has been estimated that by the year 2000 Mexico's population will have increased to 120 million, compared with today's 40 million or so. In order to avoid starvation or bankruptcy the country must, in this period, bring into cultivation an additional 25 million acres of irrigated land (compared with approximately six million now under irrigation).

For this reason Mexico is devoting great energies to making more land usable, habitable, reachable and productive. Tropical rivers are being brought under control. Hydroelectric projects in hitherto remote areas are making regional industry possible, thereby lessening the strain on agriculture. Water in the few rivers of the arid north is being husbanded to bring rich but unwatered soil into production. New farming methods, fertilization and improved seeds are being used to guarantee higher yields from the expensively created new cropland. Fetid tropical regions are being opened up through disease control and water purification. And paved roads are being pushed into remote regions where, in the past, produce had virtually no access to markets.

Meanwhile the relative size of the farming population has decreased. In Porfirio Díaz' day, half a century ago, 80 per cent of Mexico's working force was agricultural; by 1930 it was down to 70.5 per cent, and today it is only about half. Between 1930 and the present, the labor force engaged in industry, commerce and services has grown accordingly. Agricultural production is increasing at the rate of about 6 per cent a year, despite the reduction in the number of people who are engaged in it, while industrial production is growing at the same rate. In recent years the economy as a whole has been expanding at a healthy annual rate of 6 per cent.

ALL of this would seem to be for the good. Yet economists point out that a country that can use only 15 per cent of its land for agricultural purposes cannot afford to devote as much of its work force to agriculture as Mexico does, no matter how deeply farming is ingrained in the national character. The answer is industrialization.

"We are latecomers to the world economic scene," says José Hernández Delgado, director general of Nacional Financiera, Mexico's government development bank. "When Mexico was invited to the banquet of civilization the main course had already been served. We have no choice but to industrialize as rapidly as our human and material resources permit."

With the aid of private capital, both Mexican and foreign (the latter strictly regulated), and with public funds made available through governmental agencies such as Nacional Financiera, Mexico has been industrializing at a dizzy speed. In a single giant step the country has gone from a primitive farming-and-handicraft economy to one that boasts new mills for making steel, coke, cement, cellulose and paper. It has factories producing electrical appliances, equipment for farms and offices, and machinery for ginning cotton and weaving cloth; processing plants for chemicals, fertilizers, pharmaceuticals and foods; and refineries for sugar, sulphur and petroleum products.

THERE was a time when Mexicans themselves insisted that their people could do nothing but farm, that it was too difficult to train them for mechanical duties. Many foreign observers commented on the charm of "machineless Mexicans." These same people would tell the apocryphal story of Mexican laborers, at work on one of the early railroads, who were given wheelbarrows to use in carrying gravel. The workers stared at the strange vehicles (the legend runs), removed the wheels, loaded the barrows and hoisted them onto their backs.

The story is suspect. Most Mexicans—perhaps because their heritage deprived them of the wheel for so long—take to wheeled vehicles and other mechanical devices with both joy and talent. Automobiles that would have long ago been consigned to the junk heap in more advanced countries are kept running by inspired tinkering. Industrial plants that have been threatened with shutdowns because of hard-to-get parts have been saved by the ingenuity of Mexicans still new to machines. Several modern textile plants have found their best loom tenders in isolated Indian villages that have specialized in hand weaving since the days before the Conquest. The pull of the soil remains strong, however. Many textile millowners find they must shut down periodically, for at regular intervals the workers return to their villages to plant or harvest their maize.

With ox-drawn plow, a Oaxaca farmer prepares a slope for planting maize. Backward methods and poor soil keep farm yield low.

The Highway from Furrow to Factory

The land is precious to Mexicans, but not generous in its gifts. Although half the population farms, Mexico can barely manage to feed itself. To create new wealth the country is promoting another kind of revolution: the urgent industrialization of a hitherto peasant economy. Oil towns have sprung up along the Gulf Coast and factory districts may now be found in every state. Maize is still king in the bustling new Mexico, but its throne is starting to totter.

RURAL WAYSTOPS *spice the weary round of peasant life*

AT A CANTINA, workers congregate for soft drinks or tequila with lemon and salt. Most villages have at least one such café, complete with jukebox.

IN A MARKET in Oaxaca (*opposite*), farmers buy and sell produce on Saturdays. Each family sets its merchandise on the street under an awning.

A REFINING COMPLEX in Salamanca, Guanajuato, with 11 processing plants, is one of oil-rich Mexico's first major steps into the burgeoning world of petrochemicals.

BULGING TRUCKS haul cotton (*below*) from Baja California's irrigated fields to gins in Mexicali, which is now one of the world's largest cotton-processing centers.

DESERT FACTORY, a cellulose plant in Chihuahua draws water from an underground lake to turn timber into pulp for the paper industry. In Mexico industrial production is increasing at an average rate of 7 per cent a year. Average income per capita, still desperately low by U.S. standards, has more than tripled in the past 25 years.

WILLOW-LINED WATERWAY, a Xochimilco canal (*opposite*) flows by a restaurant of swoopingly modern design. Tourists dine on the flower-decked, canopied gondolas.

MANY-TIERED BULL RING, one of the two serving Mexico City, draws crowds of tourists as well as fervent *aficionados*. As in Spain, the best matadors become national idols.

DYNAMIC BUSINESSMAN of a new breed nourished by the steady expansion of consumer spending likes to work and play hard

FLYING FOR FUN, bachelor sportsman Manuel Arango of Mexico City, partner with his brothers in 11 discount stores, takes the controls of his antique Stearman biplane.

ON A BUSINESS TOUR, Arango *(above)* heads for his U.S. car in a suburban shopping center owned by the Arango brothers, who also operate the large Aurrerá store in the background.

INSPECTING THE SITE of a new Aurrerá store going up in the historic Churubusco area, where once U.S. and Mexican troops fought, Arango *(left)* chats with the architect and reviews plans.

ENJOYING A DATE with a pretty airline stewardess, María del Carmen Langenscheidt, Arango *(right)* gestures to a waiter in the café where they dine, dance and greet friends at other tables.

BACTERIOLOGIST: María Briones does laboratory research at the University of Mexico. Like her six sisters shown here, and two brothers, she is a college graduate.

A REMARKABLE FAMILY provides testimony of new freedoms for women in modern Mexico, more paths upward from poverty, and a people's stirring ambition

DOCTOR: Elba Briones de Escobar is in general practice in Mexico City. The parents of the Briones sisters were poor millers who scrimped to educate their children.

CHEMIST: Elisa Briones teaches at a Catholic school in San Luis Potosí, where the sisters grew up, and studies at the university there for a higher degree in chemistry.

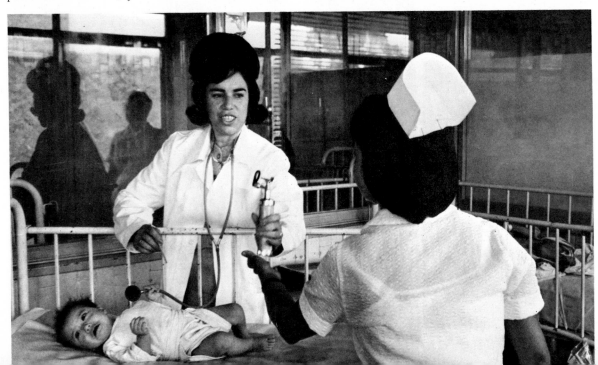

TEACHER: Graciela Briones de García teaches primary grades in San Luis Potosí. The mother of four children, she earns money to help her husband finish law school.

TECHNICIAN: Ester Briones de Venegas works for a research institute in Mexico City. Her youngest sister, Rebeca Briones, not shown here, is a medical student.

TEACHER: Raquel Briones de Luque, shown explaining subtraction in a Mexico City school, is also a biology instructor for higher grades and a hospital therapist.

PEDIATRICIAN: Carmen Briones de López *(left)*, who studied medicine on scholarships in the United States, is on the staff of a children's hospital in Mexico City.

Working intently, a Mexican girl does her lessons in the open doorway of a onetime hacienda. The decrepit structure until recently

served the farm village of Techachalco as its sole schoolhouse.

7

The Right
To Read
and Write

IN a small village in southern Mexico it is
market and fiesta day. The plaza is full of
Indians from the surrounding hills, buying,
selling, trading, lighting candles and shooting
off firecrackers in honor of the patron saint,
and drinking *aguardiente*.

At one side of the plaza is a low barracks-like
building. Seated on benches at rough wooden
tables within it are 20 Indian children, their
faces bright from scrubbing. On the walls are
pictures of Hidalgo, Morelos, Juárez, Madero
and Gustavo Díaz Ordaz. The youthful schoolmaster, dressed in clean work clothes, speaks to
the children first in their own tongue, then in
Spanish. (Ten different Indian languages are
spoken in the surrounding area, and only one
adult in five knows Spanish.) He directs them
in reading from a paperback primer, supplied
by the government. The children take turns
reading in Spanish, phrasing their words with
laborious care:

"Yesterday we were in class. The director

entered. Here we have, he said, another companion. He comes from a distant village. During recreation we played together .... He was very happy. Afterward we went to our class in history. The teacher spoke of . . . the fatherland .... Héctor asked: What is the fatherland? It is the land where we live, said Raúl. It is the place where our fathers were born, said María. It is the home of all of us, said Clara. It is all of Mexico, mountains, forests, rivers, said Luis. It is our national flag, said Rogelio. Our new companion said: In my village we think the same. It is the land, our belongings and ourselves—we all are the fatherland."

The schoolmaster gives his pupils a list of Spanish words to memorize, then walks to the door. He gestures toward the plaza.

"What they spend on firecrackers, candles and *aguardiente*," he tells a visitor, "could better be spent on their children, their school and themselves. Food, soap, books." The young man speaks without bitterness, but his visitor recalls that in this same area, not many years ago, schoolteachers were killed for preaching to the Indians against the use of *aguardiente*. It was and is an important item of trade for townsmen dealing with the Indians.

"Who is to teach these people—unless *they* do?" asks the teacher, pointing toward his class. "But half of them are away from class today because of the fiesta, and when planting time comes none of them will be here. They will all be kept home to work. And about half of them will never come back."

IN another village in another state and outside another classroom, a young woman schoolteacher stands talking to an Indian woman scarcely older than herself. The Indian woman has a baby wrapped in her *rebozo*, and with one hand she clutches a tearful eight-year-old girl who stares at the class beyond the teacher. "But *señorita*," the woman says, "I need my little girl at home. Her father and brothers work all day in the fields and need much food. I spend the entire day grinding maize and making *tortillas* and carrying water. She

can at least watch the pig and care for this one"—she pats the bundle in her arms—"for I am to have another. She has had a year of school. Too much learning hurts the head."

And in still another village classroom, another teacher is explaining to her pupils how to tell time. She shifts the hands on a cardboard clockface and the pupils wave their arms for an opportunity to recite. It is in a part of Mexico where, a thousand years ago, the ancients could tell time and accurately measure and record months and years and epochs by studying the movement of the stars. But in recent centuries time has been measured in hats. Straw-hat weaving had become a principal industry of the village. Men, women and children carried bundles of fiber on their backs, and their hands kept busy weaving the fiber into hats while they walked, gossiped or went about other activities. And they had come to say, "I guarded the cow today for two hats," or "That village is a three-hat walk from here." As the young teacher shows her pupils how to tell time, she remarks that, aside from a broken clock in the office of the village president, her own wrist watch appears to be the only timepiece in the entire village. No matter: the villagers can always come and look at her watch.

SIMILAR scenes of Mexico's struggle for education can be duplicated in all parts of the republic against a background of poverty, isolation, backwardness and linguistic confusion. Mexico shares with all nations of the world a shortage of schools and teachers, but in addition it has a host of educational problems which are peculiarly its own, and the struggle to overcome them is an arduous one.

It has been frequently pointed out that there is no single Mexican people; there are instead many Mexican peoples, a congeries of cultures, languages, beliefs, human types. The physical character of the country encourages the survival of cultural and linguistic pockets. Spanish is Mexico's official language and has been for nearly four and a half centuries—the language of government and of education, of books, magazines and newspapers. Yet language is not —or is not yet—the homogenizing and unifying element that English is in Great Britain, for example, or French in France. Almost one million Mexicans do not speak Spanish at all, and it is commonly presumed that there are many more who understand it but do not really speak it. Some 50 Indian languages and dialects are still alive and much in use.

IN more advanced countries, parental stimulus is a potent influence on the education of the young. The parents can be relied on to enforce attendance and to act as aides to the teacher when a child falters in his studies. But in Mexico today 32 per cent of all adults have not been to school; of the rest, 47 per cent never went beyond the primary level. Thus, although Mexican law requires youngsters to complete primary school, a great many families are reluctant to bring pressure on their children to fulfill the requirement. When economic stress becomes great (more than half the families in Mexico earn less than $40 monthly), it is standard practice to withdraw children from school and put them to work. Of every thousand children entering the first grade, only 22 ever complete the six grades of primary school. Parents in rural Mexico are likely to exhibit a feeling of resignation about the matter. Why, they ask, should my son not be working in the fields and helping to support the family? Of what use is it to know how to read when there is nothing to read?

Despite this, there is a deep devotion in Mexico to the basic idea of education, a devotion which is spreading through all segments of society. Twenty-five per cent of the national budget goes into education (the military, once the dominant element of national life, now gets only 10 per cent; Mexico has nearly three times as many teachers as soldiers). Year by year the amount of money spent on education has risen. And more significantly, the recognition of the importance of schools and schoolteachers is reaching into hitherto unschooled areas: the school building is often the most important building in the village, and the most influential person is the teacher.

Recently a teacher named Luis Pluma was ordered to take the position of schoolmaster in the village school of Santa Ana Acozautla, an Indian *pueblo* of 950 persons in a remote, arid part of the state of Puebla. Pluma did not like the idea. He remembered from a previous visit that the village school occupied a dark little room at the rear of the town hall, and that the pupils spent part of their time trying to kill rats by stamping on them with their bare feet. The village had begun to build a schoolhouse 15 years previously, but the man in charge of construction had erected only two walls and then had run away with the school fund.

PLUMA was told that Santa Ana Acozautla had since then built a new schoolhouse with federal aid. Dubiously, he moved to the village with his wife and two small daughters. They were delighted to find an efficient, clean, airy little school with an attached apartment for the teacher and his family. His 60 pupils were eager to be taught and their parents even more eager to help in any way they could.

"The villagers are poor people and illiterate, but they are the most sympathetic I have ever met," said Pluma. "They are proud of their school and want their children to learn, and they want to learn themselves." The villagers cleared a vegetable plot for Pluma's wife and helped her plant it. When the school pump failed they cheerfully carried water from a local well for the teacher's family. Pluma was consulted on all village matters. "They consider us their most distinguished citizens," said Pluma, "and treat us as such. We are not only happy, but proud to be here to help them."

In Santa Ana Acozautla and a thousand other villages, Mexico is struggling to overcome an old and virtually unmanageable handicap—the product of its Indian-Spanish heritage.

The Indian peoples of pre-Hispanic Mexico did not attempt to educate very many of their young. The sons of nobles were trained for leadership or the priesthood or both; others were trained to be soldiers, but the vast majority of children were given only the instruction their parents were able and willing to provide. Sixteenth Century Spain, which was to supply Mexico's first teachers in the persons of the missionary friars, had an educational system scarcely more advanced. In New Spain the friars established schools for Indians, but these were designed mainly for the sons of *caciques*, or leaders, who would in time become intermediaries between the Spanish rulers and their own people—collectors of tribute and enforcers of obedience. While the friars did valiant work in protecting the remainder of the Indians from enslavement and abuse, their educational efforts were limited largely to the teaching of crafts and Christian doctrine. Little effort was made to teach Spanish to the mass of people; the friars instead took the trouble to learn the

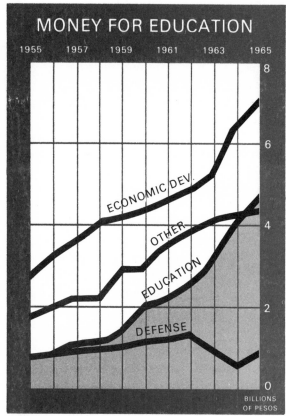

A RISING PROPORTION of the Mexican budget is devoted to education, as shown in the graph above. Spending for the military stays at approximately 10 per cent.

Indian languages, and the old tongues persisted.

After the 16th Century in New Spain the Church—not counting a few heroic individuals among the priests and friars—tended to become more preoccupied with landowning and other forms of wealth. Sharing the archconservative opinions of the landowners, it favored a *status quo* in which any enlightenment of the Indians in nonreligious matters was not only frowned upon but regarded as dangerous.

Mexico's War of Independence brought no great change in the educational system. Although many of the world's nations developed free public education systems in the 19th Century, the years brought chaos to Mexico. Benito Juárez, justly revered as the outstanding exponent of liberal thought in the Mexico of his day, had faith in schooling as the only sure salvation of his people. But Juárez was able to do little about education in the turmoil of trying to create and maintain a democratic political structure.

The constitution of 1857 called for free instruction and imposed severe strictures on the Catholic Church, which, with its own system of parochial schools, seminaries and colleges, had until then largely controlled all teaching. Juárez hoped to bring about universal secular education. A national preparatory school was established to train teachers. Towns were ordered to build primary schools, and so were the hacienda owners. But at the end of the Juárez period, only about 350,000 of Mexico's two million children were enrolled in school.

FREE public education made some progress during the long rule of Porfirio Díaz, but it did not have a high priority among Díaz' ambitions for the creation of a great modern Mexico. Of three million children of school age, no more than one in four had a school available and was able to attend it. At least 80 per cent of the population remained illiterate.

An example of the kind of schooling available in the Díaz days was once cited by Luis Cabrera, who became one of the intellectual leaders of the Revolution. As a young man, he had been employed to teach in a hacienda school. "I received as my first instructions from the administrator of the *hacienda*," he later wrote, "to teach only reading and writing and the catechism of Catholic doctrine, it being absolutely forbidden to teach arithmetic and, above all, 'those things about civic institutions which you fellows bring and which are worthless.'" A knowledge of arithmetic would inevitably undermine the system of bookkeeping by which workers were kept indebted to the employer. The teaching of government—including, as it would, constitutional rights—was regarded as subversive.

There were efforts to broaden the effectiveness of Mexican education, but many of them were on a par with the action of a onetime governor of Puebla, who decreed that henceforth it would be illegal for anyone in his state to be illiterate. There he let the matter rest.

Similarly, the new constitution of 1917 provided that primary education should be compulsory for all Mexican children. Like many other things promulgated by the federal constitution, this was an expression of hope—and of course a noble one—rather than an edict that could be obeyed. Schools were available for no more than a small fraction of Mexico's schoolage children.

THE first really important strides toward realization of Mexico's educational aspirations came in 1921 when the ministry of education, which had been abolished during the Carranza regime, was re-established by President Alvaro Obregón. José Vasconcelos, one of Mexico's most distinguished philosophers and men of letters, was named minister. He was vigorously supported by Obregón, who consistently made the federal budget for education even higher than Vasconcelos' liberal estimates. Vasconcelos built approximately a thousand schools, fostered music and dancing as a part of public education, commissioned the postrevolutionary crop of painters to adorn public buildings with murals and distributed inexpensive translations of the world's classics.

This last gesture, typical of Mexico's am-

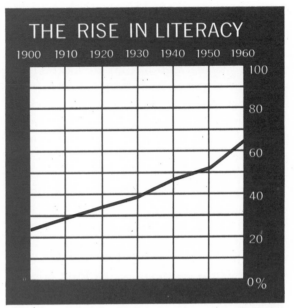

A GROWING PERCENTAGE of the Mexican people has learned to read and write through federal educational programs. The sharpest rise has occurred since 1950.

bitions, delighted Vasconcelos' backer, President Obregón. The story is told that Obregón was once stranded in an isolated community and asked an Indian its name. The Indian said he did not know, that he had lived there all his life but had never heard the name spoken. Obregón gave instructions: when they returned to Mexico City an aide should send copies of *The Dialogues of Plato* and Dante's *The Divine Comedy* to this poor illiterate Indian.

Vasconcelos managed to imbue rural teachers, underpaid though they were, with a true missionary spirit. Traveling into rural areas, the teachers helped villagers build schools, taught children in the daytime and adults at night, and counseled the villagers on political and agricultural matters as well as educational ones. More often than not their efforts were opposed by the Catholic Church and the local priest—almost always silently, but sometimes violently.

The constitution of 1917 had barred the Church from educational activities. This set off a conflict that was to cause strife in Mexico for several decades, at times almost pitching the country into another civil war.

Priests warned their parishioners that public

schools were instruments of socialism, bolshevism, Protestantism and atheism. In some rural areas teachers were murdered by superstitious Indians, who had apparently been inspired by warnings from their priests that the schoolmasters were instruments of the devil. Obregón and Vasconcelos said they would take no steps to suppress parochial schools which were still operating in spite of the law, because they felt that illegal education was better than no education. But they did object when the opening of a federal school in a hitherto schoolless area was followed immediately by the building of a parochial school. The public school would then be deserted—because of the warnings of the local priest—in favor of the parochial school. In many cases the parochial school would then be closed, leaving the area schoolless as before.

Year by year the dissension increased, and the 1920s and 1930s were marked by school burnings, guerrilla warfare, the rise of a militant Catholic underground movement and the cessation, for a time, of all church services in Mexico. In 1934, Article Three of the constitution—the section dealing with education—was rewritten and redirected to the left. "Education to be imparted by the State," ran the revised section, "shall be socialistic and, in addition to excluding all religious doctrine, it shall combat fanaticism and prejudice, for which purpose schools shall organize their teachings and activities in such a way that youth may form a rational . . . idea of the universe and social life."

FOR some time Mexico's basic educational problems tended to be obscured by disagreements over ideology and techniques. But the avowedly socialistic character of Mexican education was later modified, and in 1944 President Manuel Avila Camacho, who was both a revolutionary *and* a Catholic, took advantage of his wartime emergency powers to attack the chronic difficulty itself. "Every country," he declared, "has two kinds of enemies—those without and those within. The latter enemy within Mexico—ignorance—has given rise to

grave insufficiencies in our national life. . . ."

With this statement Avila Camacho began a campaign against illiteracy. Every literate Mexican between the ages of 18 and 60 was required to teach reading and writing to one illiterate between 6 and 40—and the latter group had to accept the teaching. Free primers and copybooks, both in Spanish and in the major Indian languages, were made available. Housewives undertook to teach their cooks; children taught their parents; business clerks taught janitors. For the first time Mexico's illiteracy rate showed a sharp drop. In the first year of the program more than 700,000 Mexicans learned to read and write. And the campaign has continued. Illiteracy today is down to 30 per cent despite the population explosion.

Jaime Torres Bodet, an outstanding Mexican poet, was the minister of education who launched the anti-illiteracy campaign. After an interval devoted to diplomacy he returned in 1958 to the same post, and soon thereafter began Mexico's most ambitious educational undertaking to date: an 11-year program to provide Mexico with all the primary schools and teachers it needs. "Education," said Torres Bodet, "is every Mexican's birthright. If need be we will make every tree a school."

FIGURES reveal that while more young Mexicans than ever before are attending school, a million still are not, with the plan at the halfway mark—chiefly because of a critical shortage of both schools and teachers. At the start of the plan a projection was made of the likely number of school-age children in 1970, and a program was laid out accordingly. During the intervening years Mexico would have to train 67,000 new teachers and build 39,000 new classrooms. Existing schools were to be rehabilitated during the same period. The cost was estimated at about $400 million.

At the same time Mexico inaugurated a program of providing materials for prefabricated schools, thereby enabling even the most poverty-stricken village to erect its own schoolhouse. Architects worked out plans for a simple steel framework that could be adapted to any building material that was locally available—brick, adobe, stone or wood—and easily assembled by local volunteer labor. The school and all its equipment, including books, phonographs, film projectors and even furniture for the teacher's apartment, is made available to the villages at less than cost; the village pays $1,760, while the government's share is approximately $2,720. Furthermore, the government extends easy credit terms to the villages to help them furnish their share. "The Revolution," said former President Adolfo López Mateos, "owes a permanent debt to the Mexican people. This is a way of reducing the debt." In the first year, 2,000 such schools were built, and Mexico is currently building new schools at the rate of one classroom every hour and a half.

AS another installment on its debt to the Mexican people, the government has begun supplying free textbooks for all the primary grades in the nation, in public and private schools alike. More than 82 million textbooks were distributed in 1960-1963 and by 1966 annual distribution reached 40 million. Although there are some objections that the books are doctrinaire, they have been effective in spreading the availability of education.

The complaint is frequently raised that Mexico's educational plans are too ambitious. In reply, educators like to cite the case of the National University in Mexico City. Seventeen years ago plans were made to shift the university from its cramped downtown quarters to a suburban campus south of the city. Land was condemned and construction begun on an educational plant to accommodate 30,000 students. Critics scoffed. They said students would never go so far away from the heart of the city to attend classes, that the same would hold true of the professors, most of whom have separate professional careers as doctors, lawyers, architects and engineers, and that there were not that many young people in Mexico who wanted a university education anyway.

But within 10 years of the dedication of its new campus, the spectacularly handsome and modern university, which charges $16 a year for tuition, had an enrollment of more than 67,000 students. Professional men today are eager for the prestige of teaching appointments. The rise in attendance at Mexico's various state universities and technical institutions has been almost as striking. In many cases the students are only one generation away from an Indian village that had no school whatsoever.

The parents of such students may have been like the bronze-skinned shoeshine boy who plies his trade on Mexico City's Paseo de la Reforma. For interested patrons he will pull from the hip pocket of his shabby cotton trousers two tattered books. One is the old red, white and green copybook of the national anti-illiteracy campaign, with which he has laboriously been teaching himself to write. The other is a worn notebook in which, he explains, "I am writing the story of my life." In awkwardly formed letters it begins: "I am an orphan. I do not remember my parents. They died when I was very young. I came from Cozumel. I hid on a fishing boat. In Veracruz I was put in jail, but they let me go. I rode with truck drivers to the capital. To Guadalajara. To Mazatlán. To Tijuana on the border. I returned to the capital. A family from Cozumel gives me a place to sleep. I am a good boxer, very strong. This is the story of my life. . . ."

WHATEVER sense of inferiority Mexicans may once have felt for their humble origins is rapidly disappearing. When facilities for it are available, the transition from hopelessness and illiteracy can be quick. One of the most illustrious families in Mexico is that of the late Don Julián Carrillo, an internationally known authority on music. The Carrillo family has produced a rector of the national university, a minister of foreign relations and a concert pianist. Don Julián, asked to explain the secret of the family's virtuosity and brilliance, replied jestingly, "It is because we have behind us two thousand years of Indians who could neither read nor write."

FILING TO CLASS, students from rural Techachalco trudge into the old hacienda which was their schoolhouse until the village raised a new building in 1960.

HOISTING A BEAM, villagers cooperate *(below)* to build Techachalco's new school. An engineer is sent by the state to supervise construction from a basic blueprint.

Raising the Mexican flag, the villagers of Techachalco dedicate

Continuing Crisis in Education

the new school, equipped with a radio, record player, movie projector, desks for 50 pupils and an apartment for the teacher and family.

Few countries face graver educational problems than Mexico. Not until the 1920s was the nation able to turn its attention from its recurring political struggles to the schooling of its people, and to this day an estimated one third of the population remains illiterate. Moreover, in another generation the fast-growing country will have more than twice its present number of citizens. Desperately, Mexico strives to meet this crucial challenge, erecting prefabricated schools in its primitive villages at the industrious rate of 19 new classrooms a day.

SOLAR OBSERVATORY, the roof of the science tower offers an ideal location for geophysicists who adjust instruments for measuring the intensity of the sun's rays.

MONUMENTAL MOSAIC by Juan O'Gorman covering the walls of the library (*opposite*) symbolically depicts Mexican cultural history from pre-Columbian times.

In the shadows of dusk, lights from classes delineate a bold pattern of steel and glass in the university's functional 1,000-foot

CAMPUS OF LIGHT, the starkly modern university buildings outside Mexico City, dedicated in 1954, are the pride of the nation

FOCAL POINT of the campus is the 15-story administration building (*left*), which towers over an outsize statue of Miguel Alemán, Mexico's president from 1946 to 1952.

BROAD SITE occupies 550 acres of former volcanic wasteland. More than 150 of Mexico's best architects and engineers worked four years to build the university.

humanities building, one of the longest concrete structures in the world. The darkened top floor is devoted to research laboratories.

EAGER ENGINEERS perch on their desks in a class in geometry. Some 7,000 students are in the engineering department.

WOULD-BE SURGEONS watch as Dr. Raul Torres Estrada (*opposite*) demonstrates operative methods in the medical school.

SCIENCE STUDENTS obtain a clear view of instructor and blackboard in a functional classroom, which is arranged with others in tiers. The louvered windows regulate the light and can be completely closed for showing motion pictures.

8

A Bold Response in the Arts

STERILE and inhospitable in many ways, the land of Mexico has always been fecund in the arts. A jade carving or temple frieze of a thousand years ago, a wall painting from Mexico's explosive postrevolutionary period or a simple, functional pot made by an Indian today —all show great plastic sensibility and an inseparability of art and life itself. ". . . only as artists," says the American writer Anita Brenner, "can Mexicans be intelligible."

The air, the light and the land of Mexico are richly evocative of whatever talent man has for design and composition in clay, in paint or in words. The colors of the landscape are strident and somber, the textures varied, the contours strange. The mood is haunting. Every aspect either assaults or challenges the senses: the overwhelming masses of the mountains, black, gray, blue and mauve; the tilted planes and arching skies of the tableland; the rude upthrust of multicolored buttes in deserts of gold, silver and lead; the high valleys and deep canyons where wind and rain have laid bare the secret colors of the earth—umber, green, sienna, pink, ocher; the tumbled confusion of cacti and gray-green agave, writhing like snakes; leafless trees burdened with bursts of scarlet flowers; monstrous vines that envelop wood and stone with their sluglike arms; brilliant orchids that glow in the deep forest; fenceposts that, Lazarus-like, take root, shed their wires, put out branches, blossom and become trees again; formations of red or gray lava, frozen in nightmare forms. The sum effect is one of magnificent disorder that calls for understanding and expression.

Mexicans have always been responsive to the challenge. Ancient pyramids assumed the form of flat-topped volcanoes. The sculpture of the earth, massive and intricate, was reflected in the carving of stone and the shaping of clay. From ancient days, the colors of flowers, insects, feathers and the earth itself have made up the Mexican palette. The strength of the light and the depth of the shadows have given incisiveness to the firm lines that bound the colors.

Artistry is found in the simplest things. Oranges, limes, tomatoes and peppers are never spilled in bins in the market, but are instead neatly arranged in carefully balanced pyramids, cones and mounds. Plumbago, jasmine and *bugambilia* are trained in graceful cascades and pillars to soften the harsh geometrical lines of humble adobe huts. Walls painted with plaster wash provide an opportunity for individual expression in pink, lime green, rust red or yellow. Home-loomed fabrics embody both tradition and the taste of the maker, whether in color or pattern or in the intricacy of the weaving.

THE arts of Mexico range in time from the monumental work of the mysterious old Olmecs, hidden in the jungle growth of Veracruz and Tabasco, to the coolly abstract work of young Mexican artists, displayed in intimate little galleries on the Calle Génova in Mexico City; from a grimly utilitarian but lavishly decorated sacrificial stone to a whimsically painted piggy bank; from the furious scenes of Mayan warriors on the walls of Bonampak to the hortatory murals of *los tres grandes,* the three modern greats: José Clemente Orozco, Diego Rivera and David Alfaro Siqueiros.

The so-called pre-Columbian art of Mexico has long been admired by archeologists and serious art scholars. In 1839 an archeologist and explorer named John L. Stephens bought the ruins of an entire Mayan city for $50. In the early 1900s a young archeologist, Edward H. Thompson, for whom the Peabody Museum at Harvard University had arranged an appointment as U.S. consul in Yucatán, bought for $75 an abandoned hacienda whose land included the old Mayan city of Chichén Itzá and its sacred well, or *cenote*. Over the years Thompson dredged the well and sent off to the museum a vast collection of Mayan artifacts, bells, masks, ceremonial bowls, jade, and cups and knife handles made of gold (recently the Peabody returned part of the collection to Mexico). Both Mexican and foreign artists have long collected pre-Columbian idols, sculpture and miscellaneous ceramics for their aesthetic value.

AMERICAN and European private collectors and antiquarians began to be seriously interested in the ancient arts of Mexico at about the time of World War I. It was a period in which the Mexicans themselves were beginning to look into their Indian heritage with curiosity and pride—a by-product of the Revolution. Collecting pre-Columbian artifacts was at first a specialty, but in recent decades it has become a rage. It is believed that at least a million dollars' worth of such pieces leave Mexico each year, almost all of them brought out illegally. Their export by unlicensed persons has been forbidden by law since 1934. But there are more than 10,000 unexplored archeological sites in Mexico (some of which may hold answers to the many mysteries in Mexico's past). To excavate them all scientifically and methodically will require many years and much money.

Meanwhile the *idoleros*, professional looters of ceremonial and burial sites, do a thriving business, not only in finding and selling the pieces but in helping the purchaser—dealer or private individual—smuggle them out of the country. There are also large-scale looting operations. Several years ago a party of Americans with a crew of 35 diggers arrived by boat at the island of Jaina, off the coast of Campeche. They carried false papers of authorization, and in the space of six weeks dug up several tons of the famous Jaina figurines and other artifacts. They sailed away with a shipment reckoned to be worth $20 million at current market prices.

That even this much of the ancient art remains is almost an accident. Spanish soldiers and priests destroyed what they could of the old culture. Pyramids, temples and idols were smashed to rubble and churches were erected on the wreckage. Three Franciscan friars claimed to have destroyed 500 temples and 20,000 images. In the Aztec holy city of Cholula, a community of modest size then as now, 300-odd temples were replaced with an equal number of churches, out of all proportion to the needs of the inhabitants. But if the Spaniards deliberately tried to destroy all trace of native art, they appreciated and carefully nurtured native artistry and skills, diverting them to the building and beautification of churches, monasteries, convents and missions.

RELIGIOUS orders vied with one another in their buildings. Augustinians tried to outdo Franciscans in the rural areas, and Jesuits tried hard to surpass the Dominicans in the cities. European styles and ideas were overlaid on the indigenous cultures. Spanish styles in baroque architecture and decoration became, when executed by Indian craftsmen, something else again. Such elaborate and fanciful schools of design as plateresque and Churrigueresque became still more lavish, just as familiar trees and flowers have a way of assuming strange new colors and habits in the soil of Mexico. Indian designs and symbols ingratiated their way into the complex patterns of European cherubim and seraphim. Figures and paintings of Christ, the Virgin and the saints became darker and darker until they appeared wholly Indian, in many instances coming to resemble pre-Hispanic idols.

If the fine points of Catholic dogma may have escaped them, the Indians at least accepted enthusiastically the outward trappings of Catholicism: the churches, the pageantry and the saints. The Spaniards and Creoles lavished material wealth on the Church. A mine-owning family in Guanajuato used powdered silver to harden bricks for its church and Málaga wine to mix the mortar. Indeed, the Indians actually gave up life itself for their new religion. The story is told that when a church was built to serve four *pueblos* of Huave Indians in the Isthmus of Tehuantepec, one man from each town volunteered to be buried alive in the walls of the church so that it would belong equally to each of the towns.

Except for church architecture and decoration, Mexican artistic talents were infrequently exercised during the colonial period. Literary expression was in the main a pale imitation of European modes. The Inquisition, which was a dominant social force in Mexico from the late 16th Century on, did not encourage creativity. The most illustrious figure in Mexican letters of the colonial era, Sister Juana Inés de la Cruz, was only nominally Mexican. Her excellent poetry was indisputably Spanish, reflecting little of the New World.

Writing did not begin to assume a Mexican character until after the separation from Spain in the early 19th Century. The struggle for freedom produced writers expressing Mexican ideas and aspirations in Mexican Spanish.

THE Revolution of 1910-1920 was to open the floodgates for all the arts. Whatever lassitude and lack of originality may heretofore have characterized Mexican culture disappeared. Young intellectuals, painters and writers attached themselves to different revolutionary leaders and became their advisers and, in later years, chroniclers of the upheaval. Young and restless painters quickly became involved as soldiers, as poster illustrators and as intriguers. Gerardo Murillo, an artist who so disliked his Spanish name that he changed it to Dr. Atl (the Aztec word for water), published *La Vanguardia,* a revolutionary journal which became a rallying point for many others.

Francisco Goitia, later famous as a mystical painter, was on General Felipe Angeles' staff; he never carried a gun and had little notion of battle tactics, but he studied the faces etched with grief and the bodies strung from the limbs of trees, and translated them into paintings. David Alfaro Siqueiros gave up the study of art to become a frontline soldier, and rose through the ranks to a captaincy.

JOSE Clemente Orozco, who was to become the most illustrious of the lot, was unable to fight because of physical disabilities, but he joined the revolutionary troops anyway and stored up a rich, macabre memory of death, destruction and debauchery which dramatically emerged in his drawings and paintings in later years. Orozco drew bitter, often savage cartoons for the popular papers, which were an important means of communication with the illiterate masses. He caricatured the old regime in his drawings—but he did not spare war-fat revolutionary generals and plundering revolutionary soldiers. He was credited with contributing to the downfall of two presidents and he found it prudent, for a time, to live abroad.

Diego Rivera, who was to acquire a reputation as the most articulate of the revolutionary painters, spent most of the years of disorder in Europe, not returning to Mexico until the country was relatively peaceful. But he soon assumed a leading role in the Syndicate of Technical Workers, Painters and Sculptors.

"We are on the side of those who seek the overthrow of an old and inhuman system," declared a typical manifesto of the syndicate, "within which you, the worker of the soil, produce riches for the overseer and politician while you starve. Within which you, worker in the city, move the wheels of industry, weave the cloth and create with your hands the modern comforts enjoyed by parasites and prostitutes, while your own body is numb with cold. Within which you, Indian soldier, heroically abandon your land and give your life in the eternal hope of liberating your race from the degradation and misery of centuries. . . .

"Not only the noble labor but the smallest expression of the physical and spiritual life of our race spring from the native [Mexican]. His admirable and extraordinarily peculiar gift of making beauty: the art of the Mexican people is the greatest and most healthy spiritual expression in the world. . . .

"We repudiate the so-called easel painting and all the [aristocratic] art of ultraintellectual circles and we glorify . . . Monumental Art because it is a public possession. . . ."

The termination of the fighting phase of the Revolution brought an upsurge of nationalism in the arts as in everything else. The creation of Mexico as a modern nation called for the glorification of all things Mexican, and the horrors and destruction of war whetted the national appetite for things of beauty. Funds were made available for the excavation and restoration of archeological sites. Dr. Atl was authorized in the early 1920s to make an exhaustive study of the popular or folk arts. In Jalisco an artist was named governor of the state. Open-air art schools were established, and school children were encouraged to paint by using their eyes and imagination as guides, instead of copying old chromos as they had in the past.

PROFESSIONAL painters were hired, at plasterers' wages, to decorate the walls of public buildings with murals. Sometimes singly and sometimes in teams they went to work. Orozco, Rivera, Siqueiros, Roberto Montenegro, Fernando Leal, Jean Charlot, Fermín Revueltas and scores of others donned overalls, took to the erection of scaffolds and experimented with mural techniques—everything from encaustic to the centuries-old and proven method of painting directly on wet plaster. More often than not they felt compelled to carry pistols while they worked: their subjects were controversial; defacement of paintings and bodily injury of the painters were constant threats.

The wall painters had been given only one instruction: the subjects must be Mexican. And Mexican they were indeed. The wars of the Conquest, of Independence, the Reform, the French imposition and the Revolution were fought over again in paint. The native myths were brought back to life; the horrors of colonial feudalism were reviewed; native industry, crafts, dances and costumes were glorified.

Rivera and Siqueiros were to give the Mexican school of painting strong overtones of communism. Even though the Mexican Revolution was unique and preceded the Bolshevik one, the Russian upheaval held a great fascination for both men. Until his death in 1957, Rivera was in and out of the Communist party; his flourishing individualism frequently did not fit the rigid specifications for a good party member and he periodically fell from grace.

Siqueiros has been more consistently linked with communism. He has spent far more time in union organization, political agitation and conspiracy than he has in painting, great as his artistic talents are. A true militant, he has been imprisoned often, most recently on the deliberately vague charge of "social dissolution." Rivera, despite his political notions, devoted his later years to precisely the kind of bourgeois paintings he had decried earlier.

Rufino Tamayo, who was to win great critical acclaim abroad, kept aloof from the turmoil of the Mexican mural painters, avoiding their "message" attitude toward art. Because he kept to himself, avoiding syndicates, manifestoes and artistic cliques, he was, until recent years, given much less attention in Mexico than his more boisterous contemporaries. After living for long periods in both New York and Paris, he returned to Mexico with the hope that he might help some of the younger painters find themselves and achieve the recognition they deserved.

PRESENT-DAY painters in Mexico are as international as they are Mexican. Their art, whether representational, figurative or abstract, is more personal than that of their predecessors. Because of the fact that they live and work in the lingering shadows of the revolutionary painters, whose flamboyant style was so easily identifiable as Mexican, their struggle for acceptance is more difficult than the struggles of young painters elsewhere. "I am not concerned with my nationality," declares the painter Juan Soriano. "I can assure you I don't carry it like a chip on my shoulder, nor do I have to remind myself daily that I am a Mexican. . . . I am Mexican without any difficulty and without worrying about it. But it wouldn't bother me in the least if I happened to have another nationality. . . . For me, the only important revolution is that of taste."

José Luis Cuevas, whose drawings have become internationally known, charges that the revolutionary and monumental tradition has burdened Mexican art with conformity, and that the more imaginative artists are concealed behind a "cactus curtain." "What I want in my country's art," says Cuevas, "are broad highways leading out to the rest of the world rather than narrow trails connecting one adobe village with another."

ALTHOUGH the Mexican government is not so active in the arts today as it was at the close of the Revolution, it still exercises a benevolent, paternal interest in them. Murals are commissioned for all new public buildings; the largest display of recent ones is on the walls of the National University outside Mexico City. Generous art scholarships are available through government agencies. The treasury department will accept works of art in lieu of cash in payment of an artist's taxes. And the works of Orozco and Rivera posthumously have been given the official character of national treasures, not to be sold without the permission of the state and never to be removed permanently from the territory of Mexico.

The Revolution was as powerful a stimulus for Mexico's writers as it was for the painters. Two entire generations of new writers sprang from it: Mariano Azuela, Martín Luis Guzmán, Gregorio López y Fuentes and José Rubén Romero in the first; Rafael Muñoz, Xavier Icaza, Mauricio Magdaleno and José Mancisidor in the second. Most of today's young writers are concerned with present-day Mexican character, behavior and problems. The Revolution is never far from the writers, since it helped to shape all of them. But, as with recent painting, contemporary writing tends to be more personal than nationalistic, more universal in viewpoint than strictly Mexican.

If the sophisticated arts have become somewhat less strident than they once were, the folk arts and crafts, which the Revolution helped revive, are steadily gaining in vitality. This is due partly to the attention paid to them by the increasing stream of tourists visiting Mexico, most of whom are eager customers for the folk arts, whether simply for cheap curios or for finely wrought silver, glassware, textiles or ceramics. Inevitably, tourist tastes have corrupted the product to some degree. Popular patterns and designs tend to be repeated endlessly. Despite this, the variety of goods offered is prodigal: papier-mâché figures from Celaya, wood carvings from Huejotzingo, lacquer ware from Michoacán, tinware from San Miguel de Allende and Pátzcuaro, whimsical clay animals and birds from Tonalá, polychrome clay figures from Metepec, black pottery from Oaxaca, fine leatherwork from Jalisco.

The Mexican government believes that the popular arts and industries are an important segment of the economy and has taken measures both to preserve them and to stimulate their further development. Federally operated museums of popular arts have been opened in various parts of the republic. Indian craftsmen are paid fair prices for their work—and prices have thus tended to become standardized. While a premium is put both on the quality of execution and on imagination, the government avoids telling the Indian craftsmen what they should make.

IT was once felt that the opening of roads and other means of communication would destroy the folk arts. They had developed as products of isolation: what the Indian needed he had either to make himself or to buy from another Indian in a nearby community. Areas tended to become self-sufficient. One village would specialize in spinning and weaving, another in ceramics and a third in *petates* (straw sleeping mats), and on market days they would exchange their goods.

Modern methods of transportation have, it is true, intruded on this old system. Beside carefully hand-wrought pottery plates and cups one now finds plastic tableware—which Indian vendors delight in bouncing on the ground to demonstrate its unbreakability. Brilliantly colored rayon ribbons and machine-made cloth are set out next to hand-loomed cottons and woolens, and racks of factory-made shoes take their place beside piles of *huaraches*, the traditional sandals. The Indian as a customer is pleased by such things. But far from killing the old crafts, communication with the outside world has stimulated them. Instead of being limited to a village market as an outlet for his goods, the Indian craftsman can now get them to the cities and to the capital itself.

INDUSTRIAL employment is a more serious threat to the arts and crafts, for almost all of them stem originally from an agricultural economy in which the peasants had at least three idle months between crops. These were months during which the Indian could exercise his craftsmanship and bring in a little money. Mexico is gradually becoming both urbanized and industrialized, and industry is eager to get skilled craftsmen—weavers in the textile mills, embroidery workers for electronic circuits. If the day comes when the Indian craftsmen are all working at industrial jobs, the admirable, imaginative native arts may disappear.

But some experts believe this may not happen. One is Daniel F. Rubín de la Borbolla, the country's authority on folk arts and for many years director of the National Museum of Popular Arts and Crafts in Mexico City. "Rural families here feel the pull to the city that rural families everywhere feel," he says, "but rural society is not disappearing here as it is elsewhere. You must remember several things about the Mexican craftsmen. The simple things give them pleasure. The crafts preserve the family as both an economic and a technical unit, which is very important to them. And above all they have an urge to create, to express themselves in their skills."

In his Mexico City home, the noted poet and archeologist Carlos Pellicer sits before his private collection of pre-Columbian art.

Enduring Images from a Dedicated Art

The motto "Art for art's sake" has never rallied Mexico's artists. From the earliest times art has served the causes both of church and government. Pre-Columbian and colonial artists dedicated themselves to carving religious statues and decorating temples and churches. Mexico's modern painters have been preachers of patriotism and social reform. Yet out of their celebrations of rural life and revolt, they have forged an unforgettable image of the nation they serve.

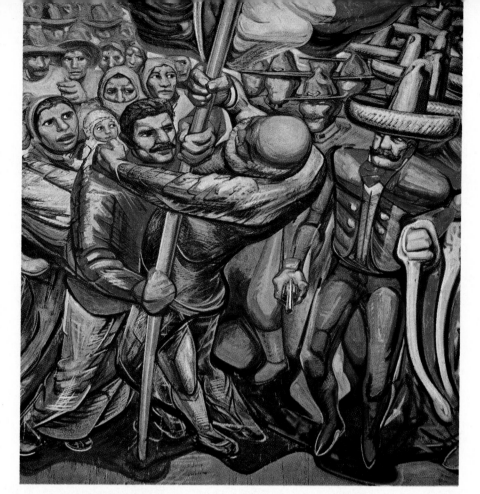

RURAL RISING nears success (*right*) as a farmer wrests the flag from his bald antagonist in this recollection of revolution by David Siqueiros.

MAYAN NOBLES stare fixedly in a temple mural (*opposite*). The Mayas' flat yet ornate style is reflected in the work of modern Mexican artists.

GAUNT MASSES (*below*) turn on their plutocratic oppressors in this apocalyptic portrayal by José Orozco, a leader among Mexico's painter-rebels.

IMPASSIONED DOCUMENTARY, a Diego Rivera mural depicts figures and forces of the Revolution. The figures with swords at upper left are Porfirio Díaz, dictator for 30 years, and Victoriano Huerta, dictator from 1913 to 1914, who was behind the murder of the reformer Francisco Madero. Madero, at right center, wears a red,

white and blue sash. Emiliano Zapata is third from right in the rear row. Pancho Villa, wearing a sombrero, is at far right center. Venustiano Carranza, president in 1914, is at far right in the bottom row. Dominating the background are foreign-owned properties and a grand hacienda, the artist's symbols of exploitation.

Fiesta: A Time of Release

ALL through the night firecrackers explode, their tiny flashes the only light in a dark, remote valley of the highlands of southern Mexico. The first glow of dawn dimly silhouettes the rude shapes of the mountain peaks. Cold mists swirl down the slopes. Along the paths into the valley come Indians, feet and legs bare, white *chamarras* clutched about their bodies, beribboned straw hats placed squarely on their heads. They carry trade goods, sacks of corn, beans or chili, stacks of pottery, live chickens, cylinders of salt, bundles of edible greens, onions and sugar-cane stalks, rolls of straw mats. In the early morning gloom they follow paths their people have followed for a thousand years or more.

In the grassy plaza of the village some musicians with homemade harps, guitars and drums gather around one of the many rude, weather-beaten crosses and begin a simple, rhythmic, repetitive tune. A garland of orchids is draped about the cross. Men in helmets made of black monkey fur, tunics of black and red cotton and sandals with high leather shin guards—all somehow suggesting the uniforms worn by European soldiers of centuries ago—gather around the cross and begin a strange shuffling dance, whistling, shaking gourd rattles and waving censers made of clay. A head man takes pieces of bright-colored cloth, waves each through the incense smoke, holds it up to the cross, mutters an incantation and places it in a green wooden box.

The performers pause occasionally to drink *aguardiente* from a pottery cup and to gaze at the firecrackers' puffs of smoke in the thin light. When the sun begins to burn through the mist they pick up their wooden box and, without ever breaking the rhythm of the shuffling dance, make their way across the plaza, stepping carefully between the squatting Indians and their trade goods, now spread haphazardly on the ground. Gradually they draw near the old church, the most imposing building in the village.

THE floor of the church is earth, hard-packed by bare feet and strewn with fresh, sweet-smelling grasses. Rays of light from windows high up in the walls punctuate the gloom, thick with the smoke of resinous copal incense. Along one wall are ranks of carved wooden *santos,* figures of saints almost life-size. Some are benignly peaceful of countenance; some exhibit eye-rolling, blood-flecked agony; and one, more crudely made than the rest, looks like one of the ancient jaguar gods. Indians kneel on the earth beneath the figures, light tiny candles, chant prayers and stop, now and then, to drink from a bottle and stare in stony contemplation.

The musicians and dancers halt before one of the *santos*. The bright-colored cloths, bits of gingham and bandannas from the wooden box, are draped on the figure, which is then lifted on a litter and carried out into the plaza. The music and the dancing continue. One of the dancers waves a red banner in time with the music. Indians come forward, touch the figure, mutter prayers and place a copper coin or a tattered peso note in a basket. A stranger asks which *santo* this is. San Miguel, says one of the men. San Sebastián, says another. San Juan, says a third, while a fourth shrugs and says, "Well, who knows?"

Another group has assembled at the door of the church. They face the east, where the sun has now cleared the mountaintops. In unison they recite a prayer in the Tzotzil language to Chultotic, the sun. Some of the elders then seat themselves at the base of the stone cross in the churchyard, solemnly pass a bottle of *aguardiente* back and forth, and bless anyone who comes to see them by placing a forefinger on the forehead and saying a few words.

This strange mixture of symbolism and religious observance, of piety and commerce, of gunpowder and alcohol is not peculiar to the Tzotzil-speaking Chamula Indians. It can be found in varying proportion in any fiesta celebrated in Mexico. The more urban the scene of the fiesta, in fact, the more bewildering the combination is likely to be.

Many of the important religious fiestas have a clear connection with the Indian past. The most notable religious holiday in Mexico is December 12, when pilgrims from all parts of the country, some walking barefoot but some even riding in Cadillacs, come to Mexico City to do honor to the Virgin of Guadalupe, patroness of all Mexicans. The Virgin of Guadalupe first appeared in 1531, 10 years after the Conquest, in a vision to a poor Indian named Juan Diego. She bade him gather roses from a rocky hill, and her image appeared on the cloak in which he gathered them. The place of the vision was the hill of Tepeyac, northeast of Mexico City; here a basilica was erected in her honor.

BEFORE the Spaniards arrived, the hill of Tepeyac had been a shrine to Tonantzín, a much-loved Aztec goddess of earth and maize. The conquerors destroyed the shrine, and its loss caused great grief among the Aztecs who survived the Conquest. It was to Archbishop Juan de Zumárraga, a man who was trying to eradicate all traces of paganism, that Juan Diego reported the vision he had seen on the hill that once had been sacred to Tonantzín. The Virgin of Guadalupe became the patroness of Indian Mexico. The names of Guadalupe and Tonantzín are still used interchangeably by some Indians of the Central Plateau.

The early missionary friars, in their zeal to

achieve conversions (it was claimed that nine million Indians were converted during the first 15 years after the Conquest), allowed their converts to bring with them their idolatry if not the idols themselves. Catholic ritual overlay a foundation of native beliefs that was seldom completely wiped out.

Many orthodox Catholics have complained that the Mexicans were never Christianized at all, and that Catholicism was, instead, Mexicanized. Wrote Mme. Calderón de la Barca, wife of the Spanish ambassador to Mexico in the early 1840s: ". . . the statues of the divinities frequently did no more than change their names from those of heathen gods to those of Christian saints . . . the poor Indian still bows before visible representations of saints and virgins as he did in former days before monstrous shapes. . . . He kneels before the bleeding image of the Savior who died for him, before the Virgin who intercedes for him; but he believes there are many Virgins, of various gifts and possessing various degrees of miraculous power and different degrees of wealth. . . ."

Among the many Mexican vexations that afflicted the Empress Carlota (who eventually lost her mind) was the strange state of religion in the empire she and the Archduke Maximilian had come to rule in 1864. "We are working," she wrote to a European friend, "to make this country Catholic, for it was not nor has it ever been so."

Historian Lucas Alamán, ultraconservative statesman and Catholic, complained more than a century ago that church festivals, far from being spiritual celebrations, were occasions for "vanity, with firecrackers, dances, plays, bullfights and cockfights, and even enclosures for playing cards and other diversions, to celebrate

CARNIVAL DEVIL, prancing with trident and standard in this drawing by Carlos Mérida, attacks men costumed as priests during the fiesta at Zaachila. In the mock battle, the devils seize and pass sentence on the priests.

at great expense the solemnities of the patron saints, to which end the Indians invested the greater part of the fruits of their toil."

Dancing, music and pageantry had all been important in pre-Christian Indian ceremonies. The missionary friars did not discourage these things, but instead attempted to adapt them to Christian purposes by adding to them incidents from the lives of the saints and from Spanish history. Where the dancers had once carried tribal standards decorated with colored paper, with brilliant feathers and with symbols of heathen gods, they now carried religious banners and figures of saints from within the church. Dances that had been performed to propitiate Tlaloc, the rain god, became ceremonies in honor of a locally favored Christian saint, but to the same end: to produce rain for the maize crop. In some localities today when this does not produce rain, the *santo* is again taken from the church, not to be honored but to be punished with a beating.

More often than not the dance becomes a pageant. Indians costumed as medieval Spaniards may take part in a dancing battle with Indians dressed up as "Moors"; the Spaniards are made to appear ridiculous, while the Moors are plainly Mexicans (in deference to history, however, the Spaniards always win). Such pageants are a hodgepodge blend of religious ritual, history and, frequently, local legend. A town's vague memory of its struggle with a bandit gang may somehow be translated into a skirmish between Mexican soldiers and foreign troops. A group of dancers garbed as priests battles a band of devils. The *santo* of one village fights the *santo* of another. Papier-mâché figures of Mickey Mouse, revolutionary generals and monsters from Hollywood movies are collectively given the character of Judas Iscariot on the Saturday of Glory (the day before Easter); they are strung with fuses and firecrackers and blown up amid prolonged hilarity.

It was the Spaniards who added firecrackers and church bells to the noise of the indigenous ceremonies. To the native instruments of wooden drum, clay flute, gourd rattle and bone rasp, they added violins and guitars.

"Where would we be," asks a cynical Mexican anthropologist, "if the Spaniards had not given us gunpowder and guitars? Mexico would not be Mexico without them."

FIESTA is a time for noise, recklessness, music, gaiety and food, and frequently for irrational behavior, with or without the help of alcohol. For the outsider it constitutes a scene of great charm and color, always picturesque but sometimes grotesque. All the senses are affected, assailed and even overcome. It is the glittering, shimmering surface of Mexican life, gaudy and illusory: it is as if the paintings of Diego Rivera and Carlos Mérida had been injected with life, given an extra dimension and set in motion. It provides an opportunity to see the well-loved and much-practiced folk dances of the country: the stately *sandunga* from the Isthmus of Tehuantepec; the noisy *huapango* of Veracruz; the flashy *jarabe tapatío* of Jalisco; the finger-snapping *jarana* of Yucatán.

The music may come from a full band, loud and brassy, from a guitar-playing, singing trio or from a lone marimba player under a laurel tree in the plaza, rippling out the liquid music of southern Mexico. There is a quality to the music that non-Mexicans can only imitate, never duplicate, no matter whether it is the serious work of the great composer Carlos Chavez or a simple folk tune. The throbbing of the ancient *huehuetl* drum is picked up by the *guitarrón*, or large guitar, and the shrill cry of the *chirimía*, or primitive flute, is echoed in the high-pitched trumpet and the falsetto voice of a tenor. The songs, like folk music everywhere, tell tales to unlettered listeners— stories of love and betrayal, bandits and heroes,

manslaughter, remorse, poverty and longing.

There may be a bullfight which may combine grace and beauty with cruelty and ugliness, depending upon the visitor's tastes, but which will always blend incredible Mexican bravado with Spanish pomp.

The noise is astonishing: explosions, bells ringing, voices singing the festive *las mañanitas*, the racket of trucks and buses bringing fiestagoers in from outlying areas. The decibels build up steadily. A dancing fraternity performs traditional steps, shaking gourds, strumming armadillo-shell guitars and chanting, "Let us dance so that on Judgment Day we'll be prepared." Blank shells are fired from pistols. Vendors of flavored ices, soft drinks and *tacos* shout of their wares. Men with clusters of gas-filled balloons and poles streaming ribbons blow whistles to encourage sales. The village band plays from the *kiosco* in the center of the plaza; a sound truck threads its way through the crowd, playing over and over again a recorded speech by the governor of the state; and from a side street comes the mechanical clangor of a merry-go-round.

THERE are mountains of food. Sidewalk stalls offer caldrons of beans and rice, stacks of *tortillas*, tripe soup (good for hangovers), rich roast pork and crisp cracklings, chicken and turkey wrapped in banana leaves and cooked with thick, spicy *mole* sauce, platters of roast kid, slices of sun-dried beef fried with peppers, fresh water shrimps and mussels, maguey worms and grasshoppers fried crisp, stalks of sugar cane for chewing, slabs of watermelon.

Eating is not confined to a single part of the day but goes on and on, as does the general din and the drinking. The peasant who takes a *trago* of raw sugar-cane alcohol at dawn to throw off the night's chill soon joins old friends to share a clay bowl or a gourd flask of *pulque* —on which, Mexicans say, one can get as drunk as 400 rabbits. Slim bottles of *aguardiente*, tequila and *mezcal* are passed back and forth. The level of intoxication is not, at first, apparent. Men hunker on the ground in the shade of a flowering tree, whispering together, laughing infrequently and softly. Then one will rise to his feet, raise his hat in the air, throw back his head and for no apparent reason howl like a coyote. The cry will be answered from another sector of the crowded square and still another.

From the corner *cantina,* where people with shoes sit at tables and drink rum or brandy or bottled beer, a flood of jukebox music spills out. The motion picture theater opens, showing an American western film; the sound track is piped outside and the thunder of hoofs is added to the babel of the plaza. From behind the canvas walls of a puppet theater come the excited cries of children.

As darkness falls, a fireworks *castillo,* or castle, is erected in the plaza; pinwheels spin, rockets rise in the air and the Mexican flag is illuminated in colored fire; and after a series of explosions the whole contraption goes dark. Country women sit on the ground, patient and immobile as the earth, watching with entranced dark eyes, patting *rebozo*-wrapped babies to sleep. Children, exhausted, stretch beside them and sleep under the laurels and the jacarandas.

THE comparative peace and quiet may be suddenly shattered by screams, shouts and the sound of running feet in a side street. In a little while it is explained: there has been a knifing, a disagreement over a dance hall girl. The men squatting under the trees with their bottles hear the news and laugh loudly, outrageously, unreasonably. They are not men generally given to hilarity, and on another occasion they would not think of laughing at another's misfortune. But the fiesta represents a complete change in their accustomed way of life, a massive shift in values.

Their lives are spent, for the most part, in silence and solitude. The character of the land, empty and inaccessible, imposes loneliness. Walls of adobe, stone, bamboo and cactus surround their homes. Suspicion and distrust build higher walls around their souls. The fiesta is a time for making a breach in the walls, for letting down the barriers, and in the process

the Mexican often goes from one extreme to the other. The humble Indian, silent, stoic, Spartan and obsequious, becomes loud, boastful and reckless. There is a quick change from penny-clutching poverty to prodigal spending, from backbreaking work to rebellious sloth. Persistent misery is exchanged for a few hours of gaiety and carelessness. The man who has been hard put to afford a measure of corn and beans buys a candle for the town *santo,* a ribbon for his wife's hair, sweets for his children and a bottle of liquor to share with friends or, late in the day, strangers.

THE Indian at fiesta time leaves trouble and solitude behind him. He feels free to laugh uproariously at matters of importance, to consider trivia with great gravity or, if the occasion arises, to spit in the eye of the governor. His reactions may explain in some measure how a nation of gentle, long-suffering people with gracious manners and soft voices has erupted so many times in the past into wars of inhuman violence in which Mexican killed Mexican with utter abandon. The fiesta is another alternative to misery.

"This is the night," writes Octavio Paz, the most penetrating contemporary analyst of the Mexican mind, "when friends who have not exchanged more than the prescribed courtesies for months, get drunk together, trade confidences, weep over the same troubles, discover they are brothers, and sometimes, to prove it, kill each other. The night is full of songs and loud cries. The lover wakes up his sweetheart with an orchestra. There are jokes and conversations from balcony to balcony, sidewalk to sidewalk. Nobody talks quietly. Hats fly in the air. Laughter and curses ring like silver pesos . . . the Mexican does not seek amusement: he seeks to escape from himself, to leap over the wall of solitude that confines him during the rest of the year. All are possessed by violence and frenzy. Their souls explode . . . this fiesta, shot through with lightning and delirium, is the brilliant reverse to our silence and apathy, our reticence and gloom."

A Pious People's Many-Sided Faith

Just as religion had many uses in the Europe of the Middle Ages, so in Mexico today faith and the Church serve a variety of purposes. To millions of devout Roman Catholics, the Church not only promises a life after death but through its rituals and feasts adorns this life as

well. The church buildings house the only art many parishioners ever see. The saints are the focus of local patriotism. In rural Mexico, church pageants are the people's theater, and religious festivals offer a leavening of merriment in a life of unrelenting toil.

MERRY INCENDIARIES at a fiesta light up the night sky by tossing firecrackers into the air around a pinwheel, which is attached to a wicker framework for fireworks.

REVERENT GIRLS dressed all in white hold candles *(left)* as they wait to take their first Communion during the nationwide festival in honor of the Virgin of Guadelupe.

141

PAPER MEN built upon frames of wire (*left*) are hung with firecrackers to make explosive effigies. At fiesta time, Judas Iscariot is a favored victim.

PAINTED BOY, his face decorated with silver (*opposite*), is made up to act in a village pageant. He takes the part of a Moor who battles the Spanish.

AIRY NURSERY for workers' children tops a Mexico City government office. Both industry and government now offer an elaborate array of social services to employees.

10

The Gap
To Be
Closed

THERE is in Mexico an innocent and felicitous tendency to mask the nation's face and conceal the workings of its complicated heart. The beauty of the land and the charms of its people, the brilliant colors and the stirring sounds combine to impair insight and understanding. So beguiled can the visitor become that he may easily overlook the fact that Mexico is a nation in travail.

Mexico is in the midst of a difficult transition from an inadequate agricultural economy to an industrial one capable of providing security for one of the world's fastest-growing populations. At the same time Mexico is trying desperately to close the gap between the extremes of wealth and poverty that have been characteristic of the country from pre-Hispanic times. The distance between rich and poor is one that in the past has generated hatred, unrest, rebellion and civil war. If Mexico is to achieve its goals this source of trouble must be eliminated. To do this, Mexico has developed a political and economic ambivalence: on the one hand it promotes a flourishing free capitalism which encourages the growth of industry; on the other it practices benevolent socialism.

The drive for industrialization has had spectacular results. A country noted for somnolence has become one of hustle and hurry. City sky-lines change overnight. Industrial parks rise on what was empty land. Evidence of new wealth is everywhere apparent—in mansions, limousines and a lavish scale of living. The number of Mexican millionaires is believed to have doubled since World War II.

MOST of the new wealth differs sharply from traditional Mexican wealth. The new millionaires are in a class by themselves. They bear little resemblance either to the old *caciques,* or leaders, who grew fat and wealthy on the spoils of war and the privileges of peace and political power, or even to the old landed aristocracy. The new men of wealth are bankers, investors, developers, industrialists and engineers. Their fortunes have risen with the bustling Mexican economy—an economy in which it is possible to get a 10 per cent yearly return on a gilt-edged investment and many times that on a speculative one. Their way of living helps give Mexico City a dramatic air of opulence.

But the prosperity of an enterprising minority cannot hide the grim and persistent poverty of a majority of the population. Only 7.3 per cent of all Mexicans earn incomes of more than $240 a month. It has been estimated that in Mexico the minimal monthly income for bare family subsistence is $60. And a recent survey showed that even in the most prosperous parts of Mexico, only 67 per cent of the families earn as much as $60 a month. In the less prosperous northern and Gulf Coast states a scant 40 per cent do so. In the central, southern and Pacific Coast states only 20 per cent of the families earn enough to meet the minimal cost of food, clothing and shelter.

In the Mezquital valley of the state of Hidalgo, 80 miles from Mexico City, 70,000 Otomi Indians live on an economic level that is still lower. The earth is parched and sterile, the landscape empty. The only vegetation is desert growth—cactus, mesquite and maguey. The last, a broad-leafed plant of the agave family, is the principal support of human life. Its fibers are made into baskets, ropes and rough cloth.

The leaves are used as fodder, roofing material and fuel. Its sap, when fermented, becomes pulque, the traditional intoxicant of Indian Mexico. Pulque takes the place of water and is drunk at all meals. It is supposed to contain vitamins to supplement an otherwise inadequate diet, and the alcoholic content helps dull the edge of misery.

In Dios Padre, a village in the Mezquital valley, lives Hipólito Ramírez, who thinks his age is about 50. With his wife, Manuela, who is about 35, and his five children he lives in a hovel that measures 10 by 15 feet. The Ramírezes share the space with a varying collection of livestock—usually a scrawny pig or two, a goat, a turkey and a starving dog. The adobe walls are a network of interlaced mesquite boughs and maguey leaves. The roof is made of maguey leaves, laid on like tiles. There is no furniture. Water for cooking is brought from a distant well (there is not enough water for bathing). The family diet consists of *tortillas,* beans, sour maize gruel, a broth made by boiling pigweed and a tea made of lemon leaves.

THE existence of the Ramírez family is measured from one market day to the next. When market day comes, the whole family trudges several dusty miles carrying loads of whatever they have to sell or barter: baskets and hanks of rope made from maguey fiber, bundles of mesquite for sale as firewood, bunches of wild herbs and chunks of limestone. With the little cash they receive for these things they buy enough maize to feed themselves for another week. If there is cash left over it may be spent on a piece of calico for Manuela to embroider and sell on the next market day. On their way home from market the Ramírez family will gather more mesquite wood, wild herbs and maguey leaves and even cattle droppings for fuel. "The land is very harsh with us," says Hipólito.

In despair, many families like the Ramírezes finally give up the land where their people have lived since pre-Hispanic times, and move to the city. Their migration accounts in large part for the massive population shift that has been going on in Mexico for the past 30 years. In this period the urban population has more than tripled while that of rural areas has gained by only about 60 per cent.

Only rarely does the move to the city improve the lot of people like the Ramírezes. If they find shelter at all—and some never do—it is either in a filthy tenement or in a makeshift hut, patched together with packing boxes, scrap lumber and tin, in one of the squatter communities that ring most Mexican cities. Here the migrants live in squalor. Their miseries are often worse than those from which they tried to escape. Disease and political demagoguery find them easy victims. Most of them are illiterate, and few have skills that can be used gainfully in an urban environment. Any work they secure is likely to be sporadic and of the most menial sort. If they fail to get any work at all, they may turn to petty crime.

THERE can be no underestimating the problem presented by the Ramírezes and the millions of families like them. In order that Mexico may achieve stability and avoid the violence of the past, these people must be raised to a higher economic and social level. They must be given a sense of decency, security and purpose. If this can be achieved, they may in time be stabilized as useful members of society and may even make their way into the growing Mexican middle class.

The middle class in Mexico—skilled workers, teachers, technicians, civil servants, clerks, managers, shopkeepers—has been increasing at a rapid rate since 1940, when the nation began to make substantial progress toward industrialization. There is no precise head count. The size of the group is measured, instead, by the number of luxury goods that it buys—automobiles, bicycles, refrigerators, telephones, sewing machines, television sets and cosmetics. But in Mexico the growth of the middle class tends also to be measured in terms of things like shoes and bread, which older, more highly developed economies tend to take for granted as

necessities of all classes. The upward-bound Mexican today shows his new status by discarding his sandals for factory-made shoes; in a recent 20-year period Mexico's shoe output increased by a staggering 3,000 per cent.

The same advancing Mexican has, quite likely, spent at least a few years of his life in a windowless adobe hovel, but he now lives in a modern apartment with light and water, and his rent is controlled by the government. He long ago gave up his straw sleeping mat; today he rests on a mattress in a proper bed. He has abandoned the peasant's pulque (both the pulque industry and the colorful old *pulquerías* where it was dispensed are disappearing) and has turned to bourgeois beer. On occasion he may still drink coffee boiled with spices in a clay pot in the old Mexican manner, but he has developed a taste for instant coffee. He may also—perhaps reluctantly—have given up *tortillas* for spongy white bread, made in a bakery from wheat flour. He surrounds himself with material possessions that he has acquired on the installment plan. And with the help of modern sanitation and medicine he tends to raise a large family of children who, with better education, may be able to rise to a still higher social level.

But however rapidly the Mexican middle class is developing, it is not growing rapidly enough to meet Mexico's needs. The country's program of high-speed industrialization has resulted in great prosperity at upper economic levels, but ironically it has aggravated poverty at lower levels. Thus, while transition from class to class is relatively easy, in 1962 only 21 per cent of the country's families had incomes of more than $120 a month. The poor are still very poor.

THE outlook for these people—at whose expense the nation creates the look of prosperity—is not, however, one of complete hopelessness. If they earn wages regularly, they are eligible to benefit from the country's vast, ambitious and truly revolutionary social security system, one of the most advanced and liberal in the world. The principle of social security was written into the constitution of 1917. Enabling legislation was adopted in 1943. In the years since, the Social Security Institute, which administers the plan, has become one of the largest, busiest branches of the government.

The beneficiary of the social security program becomes eligible for free medical and surgical care and hospitalization, for old age and death benefits, and for a host of cultural programs. He may attend adult classes in reading and writing. His wife may be given instruction in hygiene, infant care, dietetics, dressmaking, folk dancing, dramatic acting or beauty culture. In recent years the social security administration has also begun providing housing for some of its participants and hopes to provide it for many more. Life in such a housing development is, by Mexican standards, luxurious.

The Mendezes are one of the 2,500 families that live in a social security development called the Unidad Independencia in Mexico City. Vicente Mendez, 44, and his wife, María Luisa Rios, 42, have 11 children, but their oldest daughter, María, 24, is married and has an 18-month-old baby. Vicente earns $110 a month as a driver for a soft-drink bottling plant. This income places the Mendezes somewhat above the national income average, but they are a large family and used to live in two miserable rooms in a dilapidated tenement on Zaragoza Street, a slum infested by hoodlums and cheap night clubs. The cooking facilities there were wretched, and the sanitary facilities worse. The smaller children played in the gutter outside the tenement. The older girls were frequently menaced by thugs and drunkards in the street.

ALL of this changed for the Mendezes when they recently moved into the Unidad Independencia, which was built to provide decent homes for the industrial workers of nearby tenement districts. They live in a light, airy and spotlessly clean three-bedroom apartment with their own modern bathroom and kitchen. Their rent comes to only $31 a month. The Mendezes and their neighbors enjoy parklike surround-

ings and have the use of athletic fields, swimming pools and playgrounds. Nursery care is available for infants, as are kindergarten and elementary schools for the other children. There are theaters, recreation rooms, musical programs, dances, free clinics and a supermarket with regulated prices. "For us," says Vicente Mendez, "this is glory."

The administrators of social security are ambitious to bring all Mexicans into the program. At present it benefits only about 15 per cent of the population. Extending the program to the irregularly employed and to the agricultural workers who make up half of the Mexican people presents a problem for which no solution has yet been found.

WHAT sort of Mexican this subsidized life will produce remains to be seen. No one expects the products of the system to be turned into members of the middle class overnight. But most of them have become healthier, happier and more useful Mexicans. Their children may lead the way to a new Mexico.

The emblem of the Social Security Institute is an adaptation of the Mexican eagle. But instead of clutching a writhing serpent, the eagle benignly spreads its wings over a mother and child. Posters on the walls of social security buildings advise participants in the program: "Take care of yourself; Mexico needs you."

The success with which Mexico pursues the course it has set for itself is one the free world may well watch with interest. Mexico's attempts to achieve modern statehood and democracy—through land reform, education, social welfare and industrialization—may at times have been faltering. But the intentions have been unfailingly humane, the ambitions great and the need undeniable. Mexico's problems are not Mexico's alone. They are shared with other republics in the Americas and with countries throughout the world that have similar histories of exploitation and repression. Mexico's efforts to free itself from this dismal past offer a measure of hope in mankind's long struggle against despair.

A farm woman and her daughter make tortillas. Next page: Workers' homes and a modern church adjoin factories in Monterrey.

THE PROMISE of relief from widespread want is held out by the government . . .

. . . as it helps to encourage the development of an industrialized economy and a

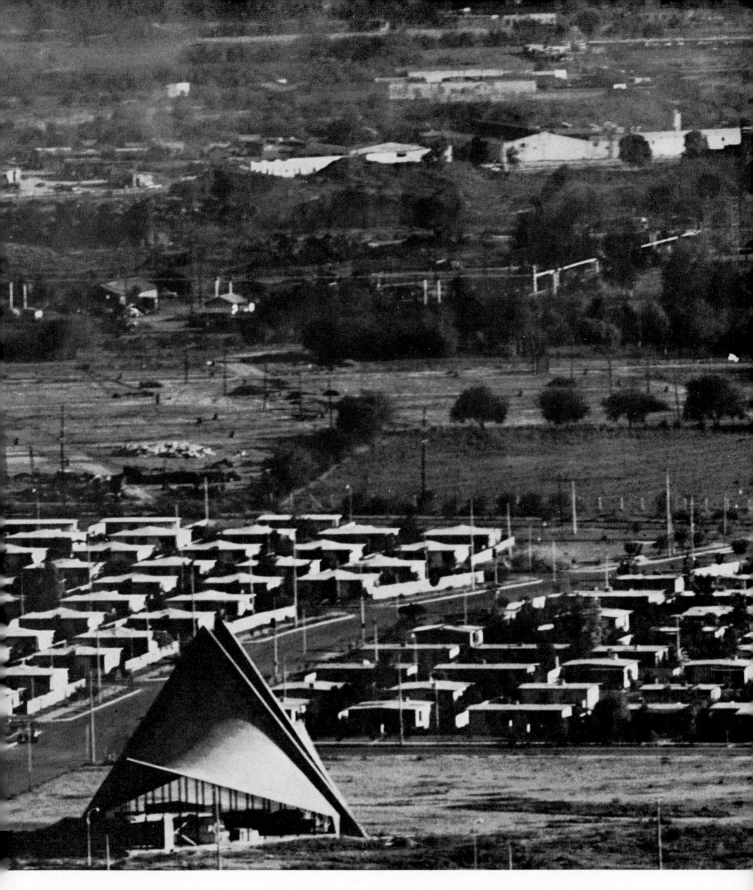

prosperous middle class that will provide a major bulwark against future unrest

Appendix

HISTORICAL DATES

B.C.
3000-1500 Nomadic tribes begin cultivation of maize (corn) in central and southeastern Mexico

A.D.
300-900 Mayan civilization flourishes in the southeast

900-1100 Toltecs, forerunners of the Aztecs, gain control and domination of the central plateau

1200-1521 Aztec Culture and Empire

1325 Founding of the Aztec capital, Tenochtitlán, on the present site of Mexico City

1502-1520 Reign of Moctezuma II

1517 Hernández de Córdoba discovers coast of Yucatán

1519 Hernán Cortés lands in Mexico

1521 Razing of Tenochtitlán by the Spanish; end of Aztec Empire

1521-1821 Spanish rule

1521 Establishment of *encomienda* system, enabling landowners to exact unwilling labor from Indians

1524 Arrival of Franciscans, first Spanish missionaries

1535 Spanish holdings in Mexico reorganized as the Viceroyalty of New Spain

1542 Passage of first of many ineffective laws intended to curb exploitation of Indians

1553 Opening of University of Mexico, first institution of higher education in North America

1557 Discovery of new silver mining process makes possible large-scale exports

1720 *Encomienda* system officially abolished, but exploitation of debt-ridden, uneducated Indians continues

1810-1811 First large-scale revolt against Spanish rule, led by Father Miguel Hidalgo y Costilla, ends in failure and Hidalgo's execution

1813-1815 Revolution continued by Father José María Morelos y Pavón. He convokes first Mexican congress, which declares the country's independence from Spain

1815 Morelos executed, guerrilla warfare continues

1821 Mexican conservatives, fearful of Spain's new liberal constitution, take over revolution under Agustín de Iturbide. Treaty signed granting independence

1822 Iturbide elected emperor

1823 Successful revolt led by Antonio López de Santa Anna and Guadalupe Victoria forces Iturbide's abdication

1824 Federal constitution promulgated. Guadalupe Victoria becomes first president

1833-1855 Santa Anna dominates Mexican affairs

1835-1836 Texas rebels declare independence

1845 Texas annexed by United States

1846-1848 War between U.S. and Mexico ends with Mexican acquiescence to loss of Texas and sale to U.S. of territory between California and Texas

1853 Santa Anna sells Mesilla Valley, the southern areas of modern Arizona and New Mexico, to U.S.

1855 Reformists oust Santa Anna

1857 Reform government promulgates new constitution which prohibits the Church from owning property and curbs privileges of army and clergy

1857-1860 Reform forces led by Benito Juárez triumph over conservatives. His government emerges deeply in debt

1861-1863 Mexico suspends debt payments. England, Spain and France occupy Veracruz. England and Spain withdraw; France occupies Mexico City

1864 Maximilian of Austria, protégé of Napoleon III, crowned emperor of Mexico

1866 U.S. demands withdrawal of French troops as Juárez continues guerrilla operations against Maximilian

1867 Napoleon withdraws support. Maximilian surrenders to Juárez and is executed

1867-1872 Juárez presidency. His efforts at reform are hampered by the country's internal dissensions

1876-1910 Presidency of Porfirio Díaz. His regime aids economic development by encouraging foreign investment, but ignores pressures for social reform

1910 Francisco Madero organizes revolt

1911 Díaz ousted, Madero assumes presidency

1913 Madero forced from office by Victoriano Huerta. Venustiano Carranza, Alvaro Obregón, Pancho Villa and Emiliano Zapata launch counterrebellion

1914 Huerta resigns. Carranza assumes leadership of the country

1915-1916 Factions war on each other: Obregón and Carranza are allied against Villa and Zapata

1917 Promulgation of the Mexican constitution

1920 Obregón overthrows Carranza, becomes president

1924-1933 As president or behind-scenes power, Plutarco Elías Calles is dominant political figure

1929 Foundation of the Partido Nacional Revolucionario, the official government party now called the Partido Revolucionario Institucional (PRI)

1934-1940 President Lázaro Cárdenas exiles Calles, steps up redistribution of land, nationalizes railways and expropriates foreign-held oil and land interests

1940-1946 Presidency of Manuel Avila Camacho

1946-1952 Presidency of Miguel Alemán. Extensive economic development marred by widespread corruption

1952-1958 President Adolfo Ruiz Cortines continues economic expansion program. Corruption curbed

1953 Woman suffrage

1958 Adolfo López Mateos elected president

1964 Chamizal border treaty signed. Gustavo Díaz Ordaz elected president

FOR FURTHER READING

CHAPTER 1: MEXICO CITY AND THE NATION

Brenner, Anita, *Your Mexican Holiday.* G. P. Putnam's Sons, 1941.

Butler, G. Paul and Erica, *Mexico.* D. Van Nostrand, 1960.

Crow, John A., *Mexico Today.* Harper and Brothers, 1957.

Downing, Todd, *The Mexican Earth.* Doubleday, 1940.

Flandrau, Charles M., *Viva Mexico!* Harper and Brothers, 1951.

Fuentes, Carlos, *Where the Air Is Clear.* Ivan Obolensky, 1960.

González Obregón, Luis, *The Streets of Mexico.* G. Fields, 1937.

Herring, Hubert and Herbert Weinstock, eds., *Renascent Mexico.* Covici-Friede, 1935.

Regler, Gustav, *A Land Bewitched; Mexico in the Shadow of the Centuries.* Putnam, London, 1955.

Romanell, Patrick, *The Making of the Mexican Mind; A Study in Recent Mexican Thought.* University of Nebraska Press, 1952.

The Texas Quarterly, Vol. II, No. 1 (Spring, 1959).

Toor, Frances, *New Guide to Mexico.* Crown, 1960.

Wilhelm, John, *Guide to All Mexico.* McGraw-Hill, 1959.

CHAPTER 2: THE LAND AND THE ANCIENT PAST

Augur, Helen, *Zapotec.* Doubleday, 1954.

Butland, Gilbert J., *Latin America, A Regional Geography.* Longmans, Green, 1960.

Gallenkamp, Charles, *Maya: The Riddle and Rediscovery of a Lost Civilization.* David McKay, 1959.

James, Preston, *Latin America.* Odyssey Press, 1959.

Verrill, A. Hyatt and Ruth, *America's Ancient Civilizations.* G. P. Putnam's Sons, 1953.

Whetten, Nathan L., *Rural Mexico.* University of Chicago Press, 1948.

Wormington, H. M., *Ancient Man in North America.* Denver Museum of Natural History, 1957.

CHAPTER 3: THE SPANISH CONQUEST

Caso, Alfonso, *The Aztecs; People of the Sun.* University of Oklahoma Press, 1958.

Cortés, Hernando, *Five Letters, 1519-1526.* R. M. McBride, 1928.

Díaz del Castillo, Bernal, *The Discovery and Conquest of Mexico.* Farrar, Straus and Cudahy, 1956.

Gruening, Ernest, *Mexico and Its Heritage.* Appleton-Century-Crofts, 1928.

Haring, C. H., *The Spanish Empire in America.* Oxford University Press, 1947.

Madariaga, Salvador de, *Hernán Cortés, Conqueror of Mexico.* Macmillan, 1941.

Morley, Sylvanus G., *The Ancient Maya.* Stanford University Press, 1956.

Parkes, Henry Bamford, *A History of Mexico.* Houghton Mifflin, 1960.

Powell, Philip Wayne, *Soldiers, Indians, and Silver: The Northward Advance of New Spain, 1550-1600.* University of California Press, 1952.

Prescott, William H., *History of the Conquest of Mexico.* Modern Library, Random House, n.d.

Vaillant, George C., *Aztecs of Mexico; Origin, Rise and Fall of the Aztec Nation.* Doubleday, 1962.

CHAPTER 4: THE REVOLUTION

Beals, Carleton, *Mexican Maze.* J. B. Lippincott, 1931.

Brenner, Anita and George R. Leighton, *The Wind That Swept Mexico; The History of the Mexican Revolution, 1910-1942.* Harper and Brothers, 1943.

Cabrera, Luis, *The Mexican Situation from a Mexican Point of View.* Washington, Confidential Agency of the Constitutionalist Government of Mexico, 1913.

Calderón de la Barca, Madame Frances, *Life in Mexico during a Residence of Two Years in That Country.* E. P. Dutton, 1946.

Callcott, Wilfrid Hardy, *Santa Anna; The Story of an Enigma Who Once Was Mexico.* University of Oklahoma Press, 1936.

Clendenen, Clarence C., *The United States and Pancho Villa.* Cornell University Press, 1961.

Cumberland, Charles C., *Mexican Revolution: Genesis under Madero.* University of Texas Press, 1952.

Roeder, Ralph, *Juárez and His Mexico, A Biographical History.* Viking, 1947.

CHAPTER 5: THE ONE-PARTY DEMOCRACY

Dulles, John W. F., *Yesterday in Mexico; A Chronicle of the Revolution, 1919-1936.* University of Texas Press, 1961.

Scott, Robert E., *Mexican Government in Transition.* University of Illinois Press, 1959.

Tannenbaum, Frank, *Mexico: The Struggle for Peace and Bread.* Alfred A. Knopf, 1950.

Tucker, William P., *The Mexican Government Today.* University of Minnesota Press, 1957.

CHAPTER 6: AGRICULTURE AND INDUSTRY

Chase, Stuart, *Mexico: A Study of Two Americas.* Macmillan, 1944.

"The *Ejido* in Mexico, A Contrast in Land Tenure," in Richard M. Highsmith, Jr., ed., *Case Studies in World Geography,* Prentice-Hall, 1961.

Lewis, Oscar, *Life in a Mexican Village: Tepoztlán Restudied.* University of Illinois Press, 1951.

Mosk, Sanford A., *Industrial Revolution in Mexico.* University of California Press, 1950.

Redfield, Robert, *Tepoztlán, A Mexican Village.* University of Chicago Press, 1930.

Senior, Clarence, *Land Reform and Democracy.* University of Florida Press, 1958.

Simpson, Eyler N., *The Ejido; Mexico's Way Out.* University of North Carolina Press, 1937.

Tannenbaum, Frank, *The Mexican Agrarian Revolution.* Macmillan, 1929.

Weatherwax, Paul, *Indian Corn in Old America.* Macmillan, 1954.

CHAPTER 7: EDUCATION

Booth, George C., *Mexico's School-Made Society.* Stanford University Press, 1941.

Frantz, Joe B., "The Provincial University in Mexico—a Personal View." *The Texas Quarterly,* Vol. II, No. 1 (Spring, 1959).

Kneller, George Frederick, *The Education of the Mexican Nation.* Columbia University Press, 1951.

Larroyo, Francisco, "Half a Century of Education in Mexico." *The Texas Quarterly,* Vol. II, No. 1 (Spring, 1959).

Sánchez, George Isidore, *Mexico: A Revolution by Education.* Viking Press, 1936.

CHAPTER 8: THE ARTS

Cetto, Max L., *Modern Architecture in Mexico.* Frederick A. Praeger, 1961.

Covarrubias, Miguel, *Indian Art of Mexico and Central America.* Alfred A. Knopf, 1957.

Covarrubias, Miguel, *Mexico South: The Isthmus of Tehuantepec.* Alfred A. Knopf, 1946.

"The Eye of Mexico," *Evergreen Review,* Vol. II, No. 7 (Winter, 1959).

Groth-Kimball, Irmgard and Franz Feuchtwanger, *The Art of Ancient Mexico.* Vanguard Press, 1954.

Hitchcock, Henry-Russell, *Latin American Architecture Since 1945.* The Museum of Modern Art, 1955.

Keleman, Pál, *Medieval American Art.* Macmillan, 1956.

Peña, Carlos González, *History of Mexican Literature.* University Press in Dallas, 1945.

Schmeckebier, Laurence E., *Modern Mexican Art.* University of Minnesota Press, 1939.

Stevenson, Robert, *Music in Mexico; A*

Historical Survey. Thomas Y. Crowell, 1952.

Twenty Centuries of Mexican Art. The Museum of Modern Art, in collaboration with the Mexican Government, 1940.

CHAPTER 9: THE FIESTA

Brenner, Anita, *Idols Behind Altars*. Payson & Clarke, 1929.

MacNutt, Francis A., *Bartholomew de las Casas; His Life, His Apostolate and His Writings*. G. P. Putnam's Sons, 1909.

Sahagún, Fray Bernadino de, *A History of Ancient Mexico*. Fisk University Press, 1932.

Séjourné, Laurette, *Burning Water; Thought and Religion in Ancient Mexico*. Grove Press, 1960.

Toor, Frances, *A Treasury of Mexican Folkways*. Crown, 1960.

CHAPTER 10: THE GAP TO BE CLOSED

Cline, Howard F., *The United States and Mexico*. Harvard University Press, 1953.

Lewis, Oscar, *Children of Sanchez*. Random House, 1961.

Lewis, Oscar, *Five Families; Mexican Case Studies in the Culture of Poverty*. Basic Books, 1959.

Simpson, Lesley Byrd, *Many Mexicos*. University of California Press, 1960.

FAMOUS MEXICAN CULTURAL FIGURES AND THEIR PRINCIPAL WORKS

ARCHITECTURE

Guerrero y Torres, Francisco	1740-1792	Baroque secular architect: Hotel Iturbide, Mexico City
Tolsá, Manuel	1757-1816	Sculptor and neoclassic architect: Palacio de Minería, Mexico City; completion of Mexico City's Catedral Metropolitana
Tresguerras, Francisco Eduardo de	1759-1833	Painter, sculptor, musician and poet, as well as architect with refined baroque style: Church of El Carmen in Celaya
Barragán, Luis	1902-	Private residences in Mexico City's Jardines del Pedregal and in the Ciudad Satélite, a suburb of Mexico City
Mora y Palomar, Enrique de la	1907-	Modern religious architecture: Church of La Purísima, Monterrey; Chapel of the Padres del Espíritu Santo, Coyoacán
Candela, Felix	1910-	Architect-engineer with expressionistic style: Church, Nuestra Señora de los Milagros, Mexico City
Lazo, Carlos	1914-1955	Co-ordinator of the construction of Mexico's University City, 1949-1954, which employed the talents of many of Mexico's leading architects including Juan O'Gorman, Gustavo Saavedra, Juan Martínez de Velasco, Mario Pani and Enrique del Moral
Alvarez, Agusto	1914-	Mexico's modern Aeropuerto Central

ART

Echave y Orio, Baltasar de (el Viejo)	c.1548-1620	Mannerist paintings with baroque touches: *Adoración de los reyes, Martyrdom of St. Apronian, Agony in the Garden*
López de Herrera, Alonso	1579-c.1648	Mannerist religious paintings: *Assumption*
Echave Ibia, Baltasar de	c.1585-c.1645	First Mexican painter to integrate landscapes into his compositions: *Immaculate Conception, Evangelists*
Juárez, Luis	c.1585-c.1645	Delicate religious paintings: *Bestowal of the Chasuble upon St. Ildefons, Virgin with St. Anne*
López de Arteaga, Sebastián	1610-1653	Vigorous baroque style: *Christ on the Cross, Incredulity of St. Thomas*
Villalpando, Cristóbal de	c.1652-1714	Colorful, imaginative religious paintings: Dome, Puebla Cathedral; Sacristy, Mexico City Cathedral (with Juan Correa)
Cabrera, Miguel	1695-1768	Leading portraitist: *Sor Juana Inés de la Cruz*. Religious paintings
Ximeno y Planes, Rafael	1761-1825	Neoclassicist; revived mural painting in Mexico: *La asunción de la virgen, El milagro del pocito*. Portraits
Velasco, José María	1840-1912	Landscapes: *Un paseo en los alrededores de México, El Valle de México, México*
Posada, José Guadalupe	1852-1913	Engravings: *Espolón contra navaja libre, Un hijo que mata a su madre, Calavera zapatista*
Atl, Dr. (Gerardo Murillo)	1875-	Theorist of communal mural work and pioneer of Mexico's artistic renaissance. New wax-crayon technique: murals in patio of Convent of San Pedro and San Pablo, Mexico City. Landscapes
Goitia, Francisco	1884-1960	Drawings and oils depicting melancholy Indian scenes: *Tata Jesucristo*
Orozco, José Clemente	1883-1949	Frescoes with social and historical themes: National Preparatory School, Mexico City; Pomona College, Claremont, California; The New School for Social Research, New York; University of Guadalajara
Rivera, Diego	1886-1957	Frescoes with social and historical themes: National Agricultural School, Chapingo; Institute of Fine Arts, Detroit; National Palace, Mexico City; Palace of Cortés, Cuernavaca
Herrán, Saturnino	1887-1918	Impressionistic, poetic landscapes and paintings of people: *El rebozo, La ofrenda, El jarabe*
Mérida, Carlos	1893-	Guatemala-born. Abstract paintings often incorporating Maya and Quiché Indian motifs: *The Sleeping Dragon, The Three Messengers*

Siqueiros, David Alfaro	1898-	Frescoes with social and historical themes: National Preparatory School, Mexico City; Escuela México, Chillán, Chile. Paintings: *El eco de un grito, El sollozo, Etnografía*
Tamayo, Rufino	1899-	Combines technique of Parisian schools with centuries-old Mexican tradition: *Open-Air School, Singing Bird, Homenaje a la raza.* Frescoes
Covarrubias, Miguel	1904-1957	Caricatures, archaeological research, book and magazine illustrations

MUSIC

Morales, Melésio	1838-1908	Operas: *Romeo y Julieta, Ildegonda, Cleopatra.* Orchestral works
Villaneuva, Felipe	1863-1893	Salon music. Opera: *Keofar*
Rosas, Juventino	1868-1894	Waltzes: *Sobre las Olas*
Carillo, Julián	1875-	Inventor of system of microtones known as the "thirteenth sound": *Prelude to Columbus.* Tone-poem: *Penumbras.* Symphonies
Ponce, Manuel	1886-1948	Orchestral works: *Chapultepec, Suite en Estilo Antiguo, Poema Elegiaco; Cantos y Danzas de los Antiguos Mexicanos.* Songs: *Estrellita*
Chávez, Carlos	1899-	Symphonies: *Sinfonía India, Sinfonía Proletaria, Sinfonía de Antígona.* Ballet: *H.P.* (Horse Power). Concertos. String quartets
Revueltas, Silvestre	1899-1940	Orchestral works: *Janitzio, Homage to García Lorca, Cuauhnáhuac.* Ballets. Chamber music
Lara, Agustín	1900-	Composer of popular songs including: *Granada, María Bonita, Farolito*
Bernal Jiménez, Miguel	1910-1957	Opera: *Tata Vasco.* Symphonic suite: *Michoacán*

LITERATURE

Cortés, Hernán	1485-1547	Letters to Emperor Charles V: *Five Letters, 1519-1526*
Díaz del Castillo, Bernal	c.1492-1581	History: *The True Story of the Conquest of Mexico*
Sahagún, Fray Bernadino de	c.1499-1590	History: *A History of Ancient Mexico*
Balbuena, Bernardo de	1568-1627	Poetry: *La grandeza mexicana*
Alarcón y Mendoza, Juan Ruiz de	1580-1639	Plays: *La verdad sospechosa, Las paredes oyen, El examen de maridos*
Sigüenza y Góngora, Carlos de	1645-1700	Poetry: *Primavera indiana.* Novel: *Infortunios de Alonso Ramírez*
Cruz, Sor Juana Inés de la	1651-1695	Plays: *Los empeños de una casa, Amor es más laberinto.* Poetry: *Sueño.* Autobiographical work: *Respuesta a Sor Filotea*
Mier, Fray Servando Teresa de	1765-1827	Autobiography: *Memorias.* History: *Historia de la revolución de Nueva España*
Fernández de Lizardi, José Joaquín	1776-1827	Novels: *The Itching Parrot, La Quijotita y su prima*
Alamán, Lucas	1792-1853	History: *Disertaciones sobre la historia de México, Historia de México*
Mora, José Luis	1794-1850	History: *México y sus revoluciones*
Pesado, José Joaquín	1801-1860	Poetry: *Los Aztecas, Rimas Amorosas*
Prieto, Guillermo	1818-1897	Autobiography: *Memorias de mis tiempos.* Poetry: *El romancero nacional, Musa Callejera.* Travel works: *Viajes de Orden Suprema*
Ramírez, Ignacio	1818-1879	Poetry: "A Josefina Pérez," "Al ámor," "A mi musa," "A Sol," "Por los desgraciados," "Por los muertos"
Sierra, Justo, the Younger	1848-1912	History: *México: su evolución social, Juárez: su obra y su tiempo.* Poetry
Acuña, Manuel	1849-1873	Poetry: "Nocturno," "Ante un cadáver," "Lágrimas," "Entonces y hoy"
Delgado, Rafael	1853-1914	Novels: *La calandria, Los parientes ricos*
Díaz Mirón, Salvador	1853-1928	Poetry: *Lascas, Astillas y triunfos*
Othón, Manuel José	1858-1906	Poetry: *Poemas Rústicos, Poesías*
Gutiérrez Nájera, Manuel	1859-1895	Poetry: "La Serenata de Schubert," "La Duquesa Job," "Mariposas." Stories: "Rip-Rip," "Historia de un peso falso"
Azuela, Mariano	1873-1952	Novels: *The Underdogs, Las moscas, Esa sangre, La maldición*
Vasconcelos, José	1881-1959	Autobiography: *Ulises Criollo.* Travel work: *La raza cósmica.* Anthropological work: *Indología.* Stories: *La sonata mágica*
Caso, Antonio	1883-1946	Philosophy: *Problemas filosóficos, La filosofía de la cultura y el materialismo histórico*
Guzmán, Martín Luis	1887-	History: *The Eagle and the Serpent, Memorias de Pancho Villa.* Novel: *La sombra del caudillo*
Reyes, Alfonso	1889-1959	Poetry: *Huellas, Ifigenia Cruel.* Stories: *El plano oblicuo.* Anthropological work: *Visión de Anáhuac.* Criticism and essays: *Simpatías y diferencias, Letras de la Nueva España*
Silva Herzog, Jesús	1893-	Economics: *El agrarismo mexicano y la reforma agraria*
López y Fuentes, Gregorio	1897-	Novels: *El Indio, Campamento*
Cosío Villegas, Daniel	1900-	History: *Historia moderna de México, Estados Unidos contra Porfirio Díaz.* Essays: *Extremos de America*
Torres Bodet, Jaime	1902-	Reminiscences: *Tiempo de arena*
Yáñez, Agustín	1904-	Novel: *Al filo del agua.* Folklore: *Flor de juegos antiguos*
Usigli, Rodolfo	1905-	Plays: *El gesticulador, Corona de sombra, Jano es una muchacha*
Paz, Octavio	1914-	Poetry: *La estación violenta.* Sociological work: *El laberinto de la soledad.* Essays: *El arco y la lyra*
Leon-Portilla, Miguel	1926-	History: *Visión de los vencidos, Los antiguos mexicanos.* Anthropological work: *La filosofía náhuatl*
Fuentes, Carlos	1929-	Novels: *La región más transparente, Las buenas conciencias*

Credits

The sources for the illustrations in this book are shown below. Credits for pictures from left to right are separated by commas, top to bottom by dashes.

Cover—Jay Maisel
8, 9—Peter Anderson from Black Star
15—N. R. Farbman
16—Felipe Chano for LIFE EN ESPAÑOL—Gerard Decaux from Globe Photos
17—Luis Lemus
18, 19—Leonard McCombe, Andar Braun
20—Jay Maisel
21—Leonard McCombe
22—Jay Maisel
23—John Lewis Stage from Lensgroup
24—Ralph Crane from Black Star
28, 29—Map by Enrico Arno
32, 33—Hector Garcia, Baker Johnson
34-37—Wayne Miller from Magnum
38—N. R. Farbman
42—Carlos Merida, reprinted with the permission of Crown Publishers, Inc., from *A Treasury of Mexican Folkways* by Frances Toor © 1947
48—Peter Anderson from Black Star
49—Juan Guzman

50, 51—Dmitri Kessel
52—Peter Anderson from Black Star
53—Inge Morath from Magnum
54, 55—Casasola
62, 63—Culver Pictures
64-69—Casasola
70—N. R. Farbman
78, 79—Antonio Halik except right; Frank J. Scherschel
80, 81—Hector Garcia, Francis Miller
82, 83—Peter Anderson from Black Star for LIFE EN ESPAÑOL
84—Peter Anderson from Black Star
85—Joern Gerdts for TIME
86, 87—Juan Guzman
88—Wallace Kirkland
95—Wallace Kirkland
96—Peter Anderson from Black Star
97—Jay Maisel
98—Alfred Eisenstaedt for LIFE EN ESPAÑOL—Joern Gerdts for TIME
99—Joern Gerdts for TIME
100—Frank J. Scherschel
101—Otto Done from Black Star

102 through 107—Peter Anderson from Black Star for LIFE EN ESPAÑOL
110, 111—Charts by Nicholas Fasciano
114, 115—Peter Anderson from Black Star for LIFE EN ESPAÑOL
116—Juan Guzman
117-121—Eliot Elisofon
122—Juan Guzman
129—Inge Morath from Magnum
130—Juan Guzman
131, 132, 133—N. R. Farbman
134—Leonard McCombe
137—Carlos Merida, reprinted with the permission of Crown Publishers, Inc., from *A Treasury of Mexican Folkways* by Frances Toor © 1947
140, 141—Juan Guzman for LIFE EN ESPAÑOL, Nacho Lopez for LIFE EN ESPAÑOL
142—Wayne Miller
143—Leonard McCombe
144—N. R. Farbman
149—Leonard McCombe
150, 151—Peter Anderson from Black Star

ACKNOWLEDGMENTS

The editors of this book are indebted to the following scholars: Dr. Frank Tannenbaum, Professor Emeritus of Latin American History, Graduate Faculty, Columbia University, Richard Weatherhead, Lecturer in History, Columbia University and Dr. Howard F. Cline, Director, Hispanic Foundation, The Library of Congress, all of whom read and commented on the entire text; and Dr. Gordon Ekholm, Curator of Mexican Archeology, Museum of Natural History, New York.

Index

✕✕✕✕

Production staff for Time Incorporated

John L. Hallenbeck (Vice President and Director of Production)

Robert E. Foy, Caroline Ferri and Robert E. Fraser

Text photocomposed under the direction of

Albert J. Dunn and Arthur J. Dunn

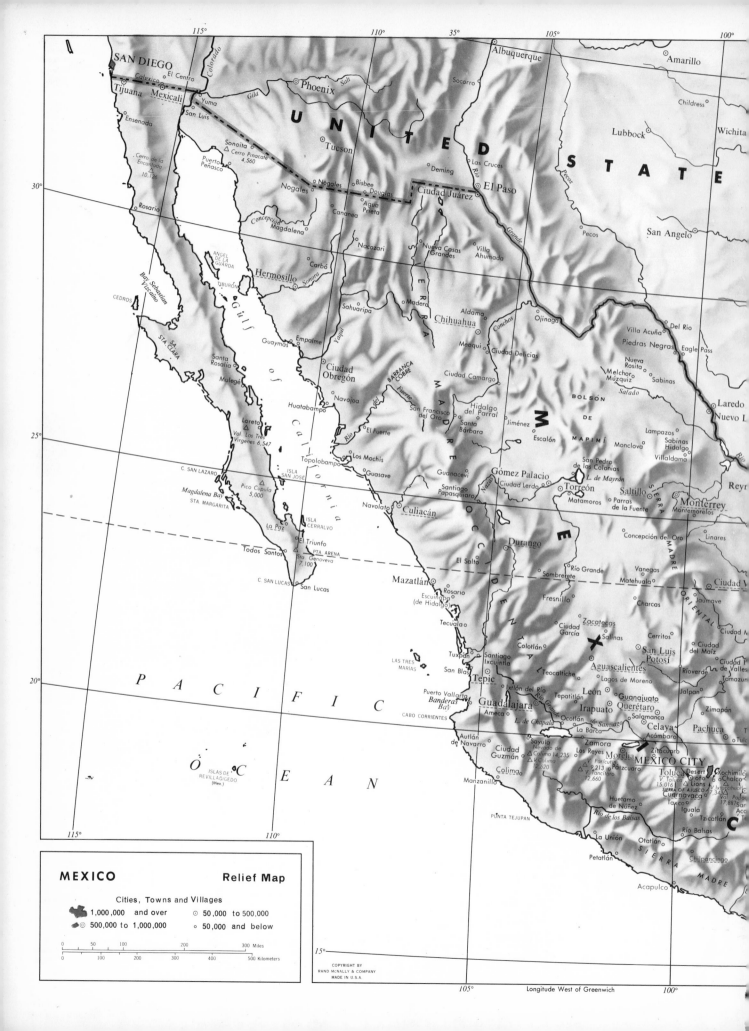